# A CHILD'S WORK

Play is the purest, most spiritual activity of man at this stage, and, at the same time, typical of human life as a whole - of the inner hidden natural life in man and all things. It gives, therefore, joy, freedom, contentment, inner and outer rest, peace with the world.
It holds the sources of all that is good. A child that plays thoroughly, with self-active determination, persevering until physical fatigue forbids, will surely be a thorough, determined man, capable of self-sacrifice for the promotion of the welfare of himself and others.

*Friedrich Froebel*

# A CHILD'S WORK
## Freedom and Play in Froebel's Educational Theory and Practice

Joachim Liebschner

THE LUTTERWORTH PRESS

CAMBRIDGE

Published by:
**The Lutterworth Press**
P O Box 60
Cambridge
CB1 2NT


ISBN 0 7188 3014 8


British Library Cataloguing in Publication Data:
A full record of the book is available from the British Library

First published 1992
Paperback edition 2001

Printed in the United Kingdom by Bookcraft

Für Biddy

und für unsere Kinder: Gordon, Anna, Tessa, Mark.

Education consists in leading man,
as a thinking, intelligent being,
growing into self-consciousness,
to a pure and unsullied, conscious
and free representation of the
inner law of Divine Unity.
*Friedrich Froebel*

# Contents

# Acknowledgements

Working at the Froebel Educational Institute, where tradition had imbued generations of students with Froebel's philosophy, it seemed imperative for me to try to study Froebel's original writings. Too much that has been said about him was written many decades ago. All manuscripts used in this book can be found in the Deutsche Akademie der Wissenschaften in Berlin. But none of it would have seen the light of day, if it had not been for the encouragement and support received over many years from Molly Brearley, the former Principal of the Froebel Educational Institute. It has been a great educational experience to have worked with her. To her I owe my most grateful thanks.

I would also like to thank Kay Davies, the former Principal of Wall Hall Training College, for her comments and suggestions after reading the manuscript and for unstinting assistance; also Shiela Smith, the former Secretary of the Education Department of the Froebel Educational Institute who typed the first manuscript. Her kindness, generous help and great patience have been essential to this book. I must thank Josie Ashton Mauro and Jill Leney for typing the final manuscript; John Maisey, the Secretary of The Incorporated Froebel Educational Institute for his unfailing assistance; and Jane Read of the Froebel Institute College's Early Childhood Collection for help with selecting of pictures reproduced in this book.

I am also grateful to the Deutsche Akademie der Wissenschaften for permission to consult Froebel's literary legacy and to Frau Dr Kirsten, Director of the Archive, and her colleagues for support and encouragement at a time when politicians in the East and West did their utmost to hamper friendly contact across the divide. My thanks also go to Professor Dr Helmut Heiland, whose discussions with me enriched my understanding of Froebel's theory of education. My parents and my brothers Helmut and Klaus and their families in Dresden provided generous support and hospitality over many years while undertaking my research. I am most grateful to them and to the trustees of the National Froebel Foundation whose financial support made publication possible.

Above all I must give thanks to Biddy, my wife. Her great love for her family provided the secure harbour from which I was able to set sail to explore, study, reflect and write. Her way of treating our children started my re-education along Froebelian lines. She was wiser, more loving and more complete than any other person I know. How we miss her. As Froebel said when his wife died: 'Only when she is no more, does one realise what treasure a true woman is'.

# Introduction

Whether we read the biographies of childhood, the records of public and private schools or the reports of the treatment of children in general during the last century, one cannot help but be dismayed at the insensitive, harsh and sometimes even callous treatment of children by adults. Even if one were to plead ignorance and custom in mitigation, we would still have to charge the adults with an extraordinary lack of imagination and compassion.

The stories of six and seven year-old children working eleven-hour shifts are well known and well documented by the Factory Inquiry Commission of 1833. We are also familiar with the fact that 10% of the workforce labouring underground were boys and girls under the age of thirteen, as recorded in the Royal Commission's Mining Report of 1840, and that some of these children were working a twelve-hour shift in total darkness. As late as 1864 we are faced with records of young children loosing parts of their fingers in production machinery because of 'sheer carelessness'.[1]

Such treatment of children was not confined to one country or one particular stratum of society. The children of the rich may not have had to work at the age of ten, but their experiences in school resulted in rebellion, mutiny and arson rather than respect for their teachers. Schools like Eton, Winchester, Marlborough and Rugby reported destruction of property by setting fire to books and desks as well as mutinous behaviour by pupils, which had to be quelled by regiments of soldiers with fixed bayonets.

In Russia, Maxim Gorky (1868-1936) had to earn his own living and fend for himself in the most sordid conditions from the age of eight onwards, following the death of his parents. In England, John Stuart Mill (1806-1873), was taught Greek at the age of three, Latin at the age of seven, logic at twelve and political economy at thirteen. He certainly was a quarter of a century ahead of his contemporaries, as he claims in his autobiography, but it also led him to contemplate suicide at the age of twenty, so devoid of feeling had his life become. In Switzerland, Carl Gustav Jung (1875-1966), though not ill-treated in school found the place so boring and detrimental to his personal growth and well-being that he managed to stay away from school for the best part of a year when he was twelve by producing convenient fainting spells.

Reading these accounts one is left with a picture of an adult society which at its worst used children like slaves for its own material gains and at its best treated them like adults and expected them to behave as such. That children needed to be treated differently because of their different make-up, because physically, intellectually, socially, emotionally, spiritually they were anything but adults and therefore needed support, care and encouragement, was quite clearly not within the intellectual grasp of the great majority of the adult population. It may not be surprising, therefore, that this period produced two of the world's most outstanding educators: Johann Heinrich Pestalozzi (1746-1827) and Friedrich Wilhelm August Froebel (1782-1852).

Much of the credit for the monumental changes which have taken place in the treatment of children during the last hundred years, and the way we teach them, must go to these two men. While Pestalozzi set the ball rolling by implementing some of Rousseau's philosophy in his school in Yverdon and awakened adult consciences to the treatment of children, Froebel developed and perfected Pestalozzi's ideas about 'how to teach' in such a way that it is no longer possible to enter a contemporary classroom without being aware of his influences.

Whether we observe children playing in the Kindergarten or being involved in creative activities in the infant school, whether we observe junior school-age children working together on a project or secondary school children learning in real-life situations, we are observing Froebelian ways of learning; ways which before Froebel's days were not part of a child's experiences in school, and some of which, within the last few years, have been enshrined in Government legislation. This alone would warrant the re-examination of the ideas of the man whose philosophy has revolutionised educational thinking since the middle of the last century.

There are, however, more pressing reasons why a fresh look at Froebel's educational ideas is so essential in our time. First of all, the old controversy between child-centred and academic education is once again under discussion. Joan Tamburrini points out[2] that the polarisation of the purposes of education for the very young 'not only militates against unbiased thinking about early childhood education but is also potentially dangerous in terms of political repercussions in pre-school provision'. The many examples given in this book will provide convincing evidence that Froebel's educational theory and practice was both child-centred and academic and ought to quell, once and for all, the more blatantly uninformed criticisms levelled against child-centred education.

The second reason is closely linked with the first one. Because of renewed pressures on teachers to raise 'academic standards' and because the value of play as a means for educating children is not understood by many, play has become one of the first casualties. Teachers attending the Conference of the Foundation of Educational Research in 1987 were dismayed to hear reports

'... of four year-olds enduring a reading-and-writing, pencil-and-paper curriculum, with limited access to outdoor play ...'[3]

As, once again, we are offering inappropriate experiences to our children in the name of early childhood education, it will be worth our while to take a fresh look at Froebel's ideas on pre-school education and especially at his theory of play. After all, he spent the last fifteen years of his life playing with children and adapting his theory on the basis of what he learned from them.

The role of the teacher, too, is again under scrutiny. While Froebel's education trains teachers to take their lead from the children and become their guide, today's practices in the classroom are becoming more and more teacher-orientated. Desforges reports that although teachers demonstrate a great deal of social responsiveness towards the children in their classrooms, the tasks which teachers provide to

> ...challenge children's problem solving skills or which stand to enhance children's intellectual autonomy are very rare. Classroom interactions about academic work are dominated by the teacher. The teacher leads and directs discussions, does most of the talking, initiates, sustains and terminates more of the activities ... [4]

Even those teachers who are committed to an approach which enables children to take more responsibility for their own learning, are not very successful. It seems difficult to provide convincing reasons for this return to a more restrictive way of education in our primary schools. Desforges suggests that as primary school teachers have only a limited knowledge of all the subjects they have to teach, such limitations may be responsible for their cautious approach to children's learning.

It is possible, however, that teachers' assessments of their children's abilities are more likely to be responsible for the return to pre-1950s teaching styles. Recent research into teachers' perceptions[5] found that teachers considered large classes, insufficient help from other adults, lack of resources and pressure from the curriculum to be their biggest problems. But the children, who were 'egocentric, immature, lacking in confidence, over-dependent, and lacking in basic skills and knowledge' were even more to blame. Teachers considered parents to be responsible for these shortcomings and suggested that as 'children absorb most by watching and listening', they are above all in need of a good teaching model. Their view of a child was that of a passive learner absorbing facts put before him. Froebel's view of a child is completely different and therefore also his views about the role of a teacher.

All these areas are under discussion in this book. Yet any attempt to isolate any one aspect of Froebel's educational theory very soon runs into difficulty because of its fragmented nature. Each thought in Froebel's writings refers to his philosophy and *Weltanschauung*, especially his belief about the nature of man. It therefore seemed right that, after introducing Froebel, the man and his life in the first chapter, the following chapter be taken up with his educational and philosophical ideas and their origins. While Kant, Hegel and Krause provided the basis for his philosophy, Pestalozzi, Arndt and Novalis provided the ideas for his educational thinking. A mixture of these two, together with his university studies plus his own observations from Nature gave rise to his overriding principle, that of the 'unity of life'.

It was Froebel's conviction '. . . that life is harmonious and perfect, that life in all its aspects is connected to make one harmonious whole.'[6] There existed 'interconnectedness' between all things: between living creatures and non-living material; between our ancestors, the present generation and future generations; between the present life and the life to come.

To Froebel it meant that there is a link between the education of children in the home, the school and the wider world. It meant that one could not separate a child's first actions from his play, nor his play from his learning at school.

But 'life-unity' was not only a matter of seeing the connection between things, a pedagogical aim, but a visible reality capable of being experienced at any moment in time. Each pedagogical event, be it a successful play activity, a new bit of learning, or a moral action by a child, constituted 'life-unity'.[7] 'Life-unity' also harboured within its meaning the notion of 'harmony'. To Froebel 'harmonious living' within the family circle was the basis of all education. Of no less importance was the harmonious classroom, where children respected the teacher and each other, and where the teacher respected the children. Froebel found harmony and unity in the arrangements of the petals of a flower, in the symmetry of a butterfly, in the crystals of precious stones which he studied as a research worker at Berlin University. He found harmony and unity in people and what they did, especially in children.

> The child is complete in himself.
>
> He is a member of universal life (The Universe), which is also complete in itself.
>
> It is his destiny to develop and to demonstrate his diversity, to comprehend the unity of his diversity, so that he may become aware of himself and the totality of all relationships around him, and to act, to live and to work accordingly.[8]
>
> The school must, at least, pave the way, for the awareness of the nature of things and their connections.[9]

As the education of a child started on the day he was born, it followed that ways had to be found to make even the very young child, the pre-school child, aware of 'the nature of things and their connections'. The Gifts, the Movement Games and Occupations and the Mother Songs are tools in aid of this goal. But before explaining the uses of these educational tools in separate chapters, Chapter Three explores Froebel's notion of play and how it changed in his life-time.

Froebel's observations of the behaviour of children on their mother's laps had made him aware that a child's activity soon changed into play when mother and child interacted. Froebel also noticed that play was above all a mental activity which required a certain amount of tension between that which was known to the child and that which was new, a continuous stimulus. This stimulus might well be the child's interest in the first place, it might also be the material which provided the challenge, but it soon became apparent that the adult was needed for the creative extension of the child's play through direct communication and interaction. Children, after all, were able to use in their play only what they had learned somewhere else. Children had to learn how to play, and parents and teachers had to help children by playing with them as well as by encouraging play among children. Froebel wrote:

Mothers and educators play games with your children as long as they find pleasure in it. Repeat them often, but play sensibly - that is, try to understand the effect and the meaning of them for the child . . . but if the child demands change, move forward with him quickly.

Therefore, you need to know a great number and variety of games and how to develop them . . . . Also come together, mothers - with your children for the sake of their play. They will learn from each other the good things; the bad things need guidance.[10]

How much guidance to provide and how much freedom to encourage has been, and still is, one of teachers' greatest problems. In Chapter Four we are made aware that Froebel does not consider the notion of freedom in opposition to authority, but as a condition to be achieved by one's own actions; something which could not be bestowed by others but which needed to be acquired by hard work.

This view, together with his view of the child as an independent, searching and creative person compelled Froebel to encourage his teachers to become facilitators, co-ordinators and guides rather than instructors and leaders. In 1817 Froebel wrote in *The Education of Man*, 'Education, instruction and teaching should in the first instance be passive and watchfully following and not dictatorial and interfering.'

Froebel's critics have used this statement more than any other to ridicule his educational theory. After all, what could be more absurd than to challenge the basic notion of the teacher as an instructor and replace it with the idea of a gardener who supports and facilitates?

Chapter Eight answers the main criticisms levelled against Froebel. Though the writings of earlier Froebel scholars are also used in this book, much of its content is based on Froebel's literary legacy in the archives of the Deutsche Akademie der Wissenschaften in Berlin. So as to provide a more mature and more complete view of Froebel's thinking, I have concentrated on unpublished diaries, letters and articles which dated from the last seventeen years of Froebel's life, the most creative period when he established the Kindergarten, invented the Gifts and wrote the Mother Songs.

Froebel's greatest contributions to educational thinking are summarised in the final chapter. Special mention is made of Froebel's ideas on the teaching of the surmise. Froebel believed that knowledge is preceded by presentiment. Only what we presume to be the case can eventually be verified by logic or the empirical sciences. Froebel argued that children operate in the same way. It was therefore important that teachers awaken and foster the surmise in children, and help them to interpret these notions. As reason and logic would not be intelligible to young children, it had to be done by the use of the symbol. Symbolic play, therefore, becomes another important educational aid.

Studying Froebel's writings one is struck by the inter-connectedness of his ideas. Nothing hangs in the air, nothing is demanded of a child, or a student for that matter, which does not fit into the total picture. Froebel always maintained that there was nothing new in his education and that he had simply brought together the ideas of others to create one whole. He does not provide a guide for teachers, nor a blue-print for parents, but, as Froebelians will testify, a philosophy which enables them to find solutions quickly, whether they are dealing with five year-olds or fifteen year-olds. No wonder his new education was taken up by teachers all over the world, soon after his death. Though the Prussian Government was undoubtedly instrumental in this.

The spread of Froebel's ideas into this country and indeed into many different parts of the globe was due in no small measure to the Kindergarten Verbot of 1851. The Prussian Government, mindful of the growth of libertarian ideas among the people and mindful of the abortive revolutions of 1848 all over Europe, no longer felt able to tolerate such subversive educational ideas as expressed in Froebel's schools and therefore closed them. Frau von Marenholtz-Bülow, one of Froebel's most active and most loyal representatives of his ideas after his death, managed to get the Verbot rescinded after ten years of protestations. But by 1860 many young women trained by Froebel and his followers had left Germany rather than compromise their convictions and give up their vocation. Kindergartens began to appear in many parts of the world: the earliest in London in 1851, followed by those in Naples and New Jersey in 1861, St Petersburg in 1868, Budapest in 1869, Detroit and Dublin in 1870, Milwaukee in 1872, Ontario in 1873, and even Tokyo in 1876.

Madame Ronge and her husband, who had been in charge of several Kindergartens in Germany, left their homeland during the time of the Kindergarten Verbot, settled in London and opened the first Kindergarten in England in Hampstead in September 1851. Frau von Marenholtz-Bülow visited England in 1854 to attend the education exhibition in St Martin's Hall in London. Her lectures on the Gifts and Froebel's new education, supported by talks by the Ronges received much attention. Charles Dickens wrote favourably and enthusiastically about it in *Household Words* in 1855. The Gifts and Occupations became commercially available and the *Mutter und Koselieder* book (*The Mother Song Book*) was translated into English.

In 1874 Madame Emilie Michaelis (1832-1904) who had been a student of Frau von Marenholtz-Bülow arrived in England and opened the first training college for Kindergarten teachers in Croydon a year later. She was appointed first Principal of the Froebel Educational Institute, founded by Madame Julia Salis Schwabe in 1892.

Existing regulations at the time made school compulsory for the over-fives, and children over three had to be admitted at the request of parents. At the turn of the century over two million infants were attending school, a quarter of whom were under five. School, in those days, was a place where children learned to sit still and to obey orders, and where they were instructed in the three Rs. Miss Bathurst, an Inspector of the Board of Education commented,

I have actually heard a baby class repeat one sound a hundred and twenty times continuously, and from fourteen to twenty times is a matter of common occurrence. With the exception of a little drill or marching between the subjects, it is an incontrovertible fact that lessons unbroken by a single manual occupation are actually in progress the whole morning in many of our baby classes in the big infant schools; and without attempting to follow further the effect on the poor child's brain,

I would most earnestly discuss the uselessness - nay, worse, the harmfulness - of the whole system.[11]

Miss Bathurst also tells us that the average number of children in the nursery classes she has visited amounts to seventy per teacher and sometimes she had found as many as a hundred in a classroom. Some of these children were hungry, cold and tired. Perched on hard benches, they fell asleep and toppled over. She continues by saying that 'discipline, so dear to the heart of the man inspectors becomes almost of necessity the end and object of a teacher's life.'

Froebel teachers, working in isolation in different parts of the country were alarmed about conditions in school. They were especially concerned about the treatment of the youngest children who were taught in exactly the same way as the older ones. In 1874 a handful of young women met at 63 Kensington Garden Square, the home of Miss Doreck, a London Headmistress, and founded The Froebel Society for the Promotion of the Kindergarten System. The influence of the work of the Froebel Society on English education goes beyond the scope of this book, but is discussed extensively in my *Foundations of Progressive Education*(The Lutterworth Press, 1991). That this influence was considerable is without question.

Rousseau, Pestalozzi, Froebel waited about a century and a half before they seriously and deeply affected our public system of education - but affect it, in the end, they did.[12]

These influences are not to be found in a scheme of instructions for teachers, nor a system to be followed, but in a particular attitude in the minds of adults concerned with the education of young children. These adults acquired a body of principles based on a philosophy which recognised the child as an essential member of the community. This respect for children, as people with rights and responsibilities according to age and aptitude, influenced the curriculum of our schools, especially the primary schools, and also the way the curriculum was being taught to a greater extent than any prescribed system could ever have done, for it placed the responsibility of 'how and what and when' to teach squarely on those who were actively involved in the task. The most successful of these teachers are those who change their practices according to the circumstances in which they find themselves without negating the principles. It is these principles, as outlined by Froebel who believed that play is a child's work, that are to be discussed in this book.

1. J. Robottom, 1986, p.110.
2. Cohen & Cohen (eds), 1988, p.12.
3. Drummond *in* Desforges (ed), 1989, p.5.
4. Desforges (ed), 1989, p.158.
5. Hughes *in* Desforges (ed), 1989, p.147.
6. Froebel MS nd 19/8/4/136-137f.
7. Klafki, 1959, p.92.
8. Froebel MS 1845 19/8/5/122-7.
9. Froebel MS 1845 19/8/6/175.
10. Froebel MS 1840 18/5/1 p.18-19.
11. Bathurst *in* Van der Eyken (ed.) 1973, p.121.
12. Bantock. 1980. p.29.

*Friedrich Froebel*

# Chapter 1
# Froebel's Life

Friedrich Wilhelm August Froebel was born on the 21 April 1782 in Oberweissbach in the Thuringian Forest, the sixth child of the village parson, Jakob Froebel. His mother died in February of the next year. Froebel wrote:

> At an early age I was introduced to the pains and pressures of the struggles in life . . . for soon after my birth my mother became ill, and after caring for my life for three quarters of a year, she died . . . . I consider this event as the one, which more or less, conditioned the manifestations of my outer life . . . . I was now left in the hands of servants . . . and my older brothers and sisters . . . .[1]

Of his older five siblings, August (born 1766), Christoph (born 1768), Christian (born 1770), Juliane (born 1774) and Traugott (born 1778), only Traugott can be considered a play-companion of Friedrich Froebel, though, as we shall see, a deep friendship soon developed between Friedrich and Christoph.

After a lapse of two years, his father married again. His step-mother surrounded him with love and care which the child reciprocated warmly. Such joy, however, was not to last for long. After the arrival of the step-mother's first child, Friedrich no longer enjoyed her affection. Love changed to indifference and indifference to estrangement when she began to address him in the third person rather than the familiar 'Du'. His brother Christoph, fourteen years older, now became his closest friend. Christoph's theological studies at the university, however, allowed him to care for his younger brother only during the holidays.

> During those meaningful and glorious years of childhood, when the world reveals its secrets to the child, . . . my spirit was prevented from making itself manifest. Child-like adults did not guide the development of a mind now trying to break its chains of subconsciousness; I was not allowed to know myself in childish play.[2]

The spiritual atmosphere in the parsonage was determined by the literal interpretation of the Bible, where a hardworking and dogmatic pastor had no time nor inclination to consider the Holy Word in any other way. Friedrich Froebel, who like everybody else in the household attended daily Morning and Evening Prayers as well as Sunday Services, soon became acquainted with a religion which demanded strict adherence to the catechism and a belief in hell-fire. His diary entries of 1811 recall a childhood filled with an oppressive fear of a child's inability 'to be good' and a conviction that the adults must be right when they tell him that he is a thoroughly bad boy.

Bereft of love and confined to the parsonage garden, surrounded by a high brick wall, the flowers and weeds, the beetles and ants beneath him and the sun and the rain, the birds and the fleeting clouds above him, became his trusted friends. A friendship developed which lasted all his life and which formed the basis for his educational ideas, for, as we shall see, he believed that the 'laws of nature are also the laws of education'.

Not until the child was eleven years of age did Froebel's life change for the better. His maternal uncle, the gentle pastor of Stadtilm, had long noticed that Friedrich's home was not the most congenial place for the upbringing of his nephew. He managed to persuade his brother-in-law to let him take on the care and education of Friedrich and in 1793 took him into his own home. Froebel, for the first time in his life, was free to enjoy the company of friends of his own age, free to explore the countryside and free to argue and to question the assumptions of adults. While his father had taught him about the justice of God, his uncle revealed to him the love of God, not only in discussion, but also by the way he treated young Friedrich.

Froebel left Elementary School when he was fifteen. By this time he had acquired a certain liking for mathematics and a love for nature. To find an apprenticeship for him which might combine these two inclinations was not easy, but a solution presented itself when a forester accepted him for a three-year training. Froebel's responsibilities included the care of the trees and the animals as well as the undertaking of measurements needed for letting out plots of land to foresters, farmers and huntsmen. Unfortunately, his master did not care much about the training of his apprentice. Froebel was left to his own devices and after his day's work spent his evenings studying botany and mathematics in the extensive library of his host. In the spring of 1799 Froebel asked for release from his contract, even though his three-year apprenticeship had not been completed. Froebel believed that a further stay would not add to any knowledge he had so far acquired. The testimonial which his master provided did not please Froebel's father when he returned home. The adults responsible for young Friedrich were at a loss to know what to do with him next.

At that time his brother Traugott was studying at the University in Jena and during one of his visits Friedrich decided that the continuation of his private studies in botany and mathematics ought to take place there. Friedrich's mother had left him a small legacy and this was used to finance his studies, not without prolonged objections from his father. Thanks to Froebel's older brothers this new venture got under way.

Froebel was full of enthusiasm and eager to learn, but ill prepared for what was to follow. Not only was his academic knowledge insufficient for the demands of a university, his lack of childhood companions had also produced a social ineptitude which prevented him from making friends and enjoying extra-curricular activities. His expectations too were not fulfilled. Even at this early age, (Froebel was now seventeen) he was looking for a general law which could be used to explain most, if not all, natural phenomena. Botany and mathematics ought to be studied together, Froebel believed, but he also took arithmetic, algebra, geometry, mineralogy, natural history, physics, chemistry and architecture. If the detailed study of a subject created too many difficulties, he still carried on with it, just in case it would contribute to the solution of the overall pattern. By his own estimation, Froebel gained little from this experience,[3] yet, there was progress in one area of his thinking. Froebel's comments about his botany teacher are of particular interest. He writes in his autobiography:

> In botany I had a clear-sighted, kind-hearted teacher (Batsch). His natural system of botany gave me great satisfaction . . . . My view of nature *as one whole* became by this means substantially clearer, and my love for the observation of Nature in detail became more animated. I shall always think of him with gratitude . . . .
>
> Two principles that he enunciated seized upon me with special force, and seemed to me valid. The first was the conception of the mutual relationship of all animals, extending like a network in all directions; and the second was that the skeleton or bony framework of fishes, birds, and men was one and the same plan . . . .
>
> Invariably, whenever I grasped the interconnection and unity of phenomena, I felt the longings of my spirit and my soul were fulfilled.[4]

The study of comparative anatomy and physiology to which Froebel refers, had reached new heights through the work of Hunter (1728-1793) and Cuvier (1769-1832). The similarities of bone-structures in different species seemed to indicate a continuous link from creation to creation and to one creator. Even as a young man, Froebel was searching for the unity of things, for order, for a system which would provide the answer to the secret behind the universe. It is the beginning of his search for the 'unity of life' which became the main philosophical idea in his educational theory and practice.

After almost two years' study Froebel's life as a student came to an end. His generosity got him sent to the university prison for nine weeks. He had lent his brother Traugott some money which was not repaid in time for Froebel to pay his own bills. His landlord took him to court and Froebel was not allowed to go free until his father had agreed to pay his son's bills. This incident worsened Friedrich's relationship with his father to such an extent that after his return home, he seriously considered emigrating to America or Russia.

Towards the end of the same year (1801), Froebel's father fell seriously ill and asked Friedrich to return home to help him with his parish affairs. During those few months father and son got to know and appreciate each other through their common activities. Froebel in later life referred to this episode with gratitude because it had afforded him the opportunity to find harmony with his father before his death. So it was with the peace of mind of a prodigal son that Froebel accompanied his father's remains on a cold and stormy day to his last resting place.

His father died in the spring of 1802 and although Froebel maintained contact with his brothers and sisters - especially with Christoph, his childhood mentor and with Christian, who eventually shared his life's work - he rarely went home again. The early loss of his mother and a home which lacked love and security were probably responsible for Froebel's over-riding aim and purpose in life: to nourish and foster family life.

For the next few years Froebel earned his living by working as a farm-labourer, land surveyor, bursar and farm manager in South and North Germany. These were hard times in terms of poor wages, and hard task masters, but Froebel used every opportunity to learn from his activities, from his fellow-man and from his books in the evenings. Though he never complained about the jobs he was doing, they never completely satisfied him. He was looking for a post where his inner life could run side by side with his external activities. He wanted a calling, not just a means of earning a living. He reached the conclusion that architecture might be such a calling. Events took a different turn and yet seem to have been indicated by Froebel's farewell words written for his friend, a young and intelligent farm-manager with whom Froebel had worked for a year. He wrote:

> May life provide you with a secure home and a loving wife. May it drive me on and give me just enough time, always to appreciate the relationship between my inner life and the world. You provide the daily bread for men; my aim is to give man the means to find himself.[5]

It is not surprising then, that, soon after Froebel had arrived in Frankfurt to study architecture, he found himself teaching in a school headed by a teacher trained by Pestalozzi.

In the wake of the French Revolution, Frankfurt had become the seat of German liberalism. Conservative political thinking was changing, *Gedankenfreiheit* was the watchword, Jews were allowed to buy property anywhere in the town and were no longer restricted to living in a particular street. Talk was of the welfare of the community rather than the gain of individuals. These changes also affected education. Anton Gruner, a young teacher and disciple of Pestalozzi had been appointed headteacher of the newly founded Experimental School in Frankfurt, where pupils were educated in accord with Pestalozzi's educational principles. Gruner met Froebel during a discussion evening of young intellectuals in the city, was impressed with his practical knowledge of mathematics and the natural sciences, but especially with his searching for the purpose of life. Gruner persuaded Froebel to join his school and he eventually accepted. Froebel was put in charge of a class of 40 boys. On the 26 August 1805 he wrote to his brother Christoph:

> I have to tell you how much I enjoy my new occupation. From the very first hour, the children were not strangers to me. It seemed as if I had been a teacher for a long time and been born for the job . . . . You should see me in my work, how happy I am . . . . This happiness is derived from the knowledge of the high purpose of my

activity: the education of men - but also because of the children's love and affection towards me.

The method of teaching in the school was based on Pestalozzi's ideas. Froebel's discussion with Gruner and the staff as well as his study of letters by and articles about the Swiss educator inspired Froebel to such an extent that he decided to visit Pestalozzi in his school in Yverdon. There was a problem of finance, but this was solved by Caroline von Holzhausen, the thirty-one year-old wife of a rich aristocratic landowner, who was looking for a private tutor for her sons aged eleven, eight and six. Karl, the eldest, especially gave cause for concern because of his careless and hard-hearted attitudes. Froebel was recommended to her and their first meeting probably laid the foundation for Froebel's idea that 'Mother is the child's most important educator'. Frau von Holzhausen's deep concern for the well-being of her children, especially her attempts to rectify Karl's weakness, and the young educator's attempts to interpret these actions and to find remedies for them, built bridges between these two people which joined them in common endeavour for many years. Froebel found a warm and understanding listener in Frau von Holzhausen when talking about his own oppressed childhood. It is likely that much inner hurt saw the light of day for the first time. Such mutual trust led Froebel eventually to see in Frau von Holzhausen the ideal mother, a symbol of motherhood. Frau von Holzhausen, impressed with Froebel's fresh and open face, his enthusiastic idealism and his first encounter with her children, free of all falsehood, was convinced that such a man would be an excellent tutor for her children. She paid for his foot-journey to Switzerland with the proviso that he would send her frequent reports about Pestalozzi's ways of teaching and how it affected him. Only one of these letters has survived, but is sufficient to indicate the great friendship which united these two people. He used the familiar *Freundin* to address his employer.

The visit to Pestalozzi, undertaken in the summer holidays of 1805, became another mile-stone in Froebel's life. Although Froebel was critical of some of the practices carried out in the school by some of the teachers, he considered Pestalozzi to be his spiritual father in educational matters. Froebel was impressed with the mobile class-system, where pupils according to ability in different subjects, moved from one class to another, a practice which Froebel eventually adopted in his own school in Keilhau. He was not in agreement, however, with the way subject matter was divided and reduced to its smallest parts, as in his opinion this destroyed the natural order and cohesion of things.

After his return from Yverdon Froebel returned to Gruner's school for a short time, until, in 1806, he was able to devote all his time to the Holzhausen children and became their tutor and educator. It was part of the condition of his accepting the job that he and the children lived away from the main house. The relationship between the parents was tense, Herr von Holzhausen was a rather insensitive and overbearing man, and the two older boys were in the process of following his example rather than that of their mother. There was still plenty of contact with the parents, especially their mother, but Froebel and the children lived, worked and slept in a small house in the grounds of the estate.

The friendship between Froebel and Caroline von Holzhausen - his spiritual wife, *Seelengattin* as he addressed her by 1808 - deepened and changed. The suggestion, in 1806, by Froebel and Caroline von Holzhausen that the two older boys should live and learn with Froebel and Pestalozzi in Yverdon was at first rejected by their conservative-minded father. When agreement was reached two years later, Froebel was delighted, not only because he was convinced that the children would gain from this experience and he himself could study under Pestalozzi to perfect his skills as a teacher, but probably also because, even if subconsciously, he was able to withdraw from a deepening relationship which could never have outward expression.

When Froebel arrived in Yverdon in 1808, Pestalozzi's institution enjoyed the most creative period of its existence. Men like Niederer, Schmid, Nageli, Krusi, were interpreting Pestalozzi's ideas so successfully that teachers from many parts of central Europe came to study the new methods. The Prussian Ministry of Education was seconding their teachers to study under Pestalozzi, while philosophers like Humboldt supported the new education in lectures and writings. The Holzhausen children enthusiastically wrote to their parents about their experiences. Froebel was deeply impressed with what he saw and by the daily discussions he had with Pestalozzi. Pestalozzi's idea to give equal weight to a child's physical, moral and intellectual development, striving for a total and harmonious education, also eventually became Froebel's educational aim. But mother-love and father-love, so Pestalozzi believed, were a prerequisite for the success of such an education.

Towards the end of his stay in Yverdon, Froebel wrote two letters to the Duchess of Schwarzburg-Rudolstadt whom he knew to be sympathetic to new ideas in education (1 May and 13 June 1810), providing the outline of a plan for the re-organisation of schools in her dukedom. His plan differentiates between the ordered and planned education in school and the free education in the home. He believed that teachers were bound to influence the education in the home because of the trust and respect which teachers, through their work with children will have gained among parents. Froebel recommended to the education authorities of her dukedom not to publish a common syllabus, but instead suggestions as guidelines from which headteachers and teachers can formulate, with the help and advice of the school-inspectors, their own syllabuses suitable for their children and based on the reflections of their own local experiences. Many of the educational ideas contained in these letters are based on the *Mother Book* written by Krusi, one of Pestalozzi's teachers, in co-operation with Pestalozzi. However, Froebel goes beyond the suggestions outlined in the book and thus initiates one major part of his life's work, his concern for pre-school education.

The Pestalozzi-Krusi *Mother Book* places the responsibility of pre-school education squarely in the hands of mothers, as such education is a matter of the heart and not the mind. Froebel, although supporting the fundamentals of the book, is already of the opinion that an education, even for the very young child not yet at school, needs skills which mothers and fathers do not 'instinctively' possess. He therefore advocates in his letter to the Duchess of Schwarzburg-Rudolstadt, that mothers and fathers should meet on Sundays, with parsons and teachers, in order to discuss the development of children up to school age, thus achieving a popular education where mothers and fathers acquire understanding by discussion.

Froebel's plans were studied carefully by the county's administrators and although some changes were made in the schools, Froebel was never invited to help.

Disagreements among the Yverdon staff which had been voiced for some time during Pestalozzi's after-supper talks, were coming to a head in 1810. The institute had just undergone a School Inspection which was very critical of the pupils' achievements. Niederer and Schmid were the two main exponents in this controversy. Froebel became disillusioned and tried not to get involved, but eventually sided with Schmid against Niederer and Pestalozzi. Froebel's main criticism was directed against the slavish adherence to teaching methods especially when applied to children below the age of seven.[6] Froebel was aiming for a more 'natural, livelier and childlike way of teaching' for the younger children. But there was also the basic difference between the empiricist and the idealist. Pestalozzi saw man as he appeared to be and dealt with his present problems, while Froebel had begun to see man as an eternal being whose potential needed to be fostered. The break between Froebel and Pestalozzi became inevitable and in the autumn of 1810 Froebel left Yverdon. Fortunately the two men separated without animosity and Froebel never ceased to acknowledge his debt to the wise and humble Swiss educator.

On his return to his former position as tutor to the Holzhausen children, Froebel agreed to remain there until Karl's entry into university in 1812. But in less than six months he gave notice to terminate his contract on the grounds that he had to complete his own studies at the University in Göttingen. Judging from his diary entries, however, it is almost certain that the real reason was Caroline von Holzhausen's and Froebel's deepening affection and love for each other. According to Froebel's biographer Erika Hoffman,[7] it is quite possible to construe from these diary entries that Froebel was the father of Caroline's son born in March 1812. Yet it is more probable that the improvement in the relationship between the Holzhausen parents from the beginning of 1811 made Froebel's love-relationship with Caroline less tenable than before. As long as Caroline was openly neglected by her husband, Froebel probably saw no ill in this relationship. On the contrary, judging by the standards of the time, such behaviour would not only be acceptable, but might be considered of benefit to both parties. This was no longer the case after the reconciliation of the marriage partners.

The hurt and pain this separation produced seems to have been felt equally strongly on both sides. Correspondence continued for many years and not until 1816 did Caroline, overcome by guilt and shame, break the relationship. Such guilt never filled Froebel's heart. His idealism, which still allowed him to see in Caroline his spiritual wife though separated from her physically, could never accept church dogma which took no account of individual circumstances. Even after Froebel was married, Caroline von Holzhausen played a prominent part in his thinking. In his often quoted 'Letter to the Women in Keilhau' of 1831, the idealised Caroline provided the focal point.

When, in the summer of 1812, Froebel enrolled at Göttingen University, students were trying to emulate the humanistic ideals of the time. 'To find thyself' and to perfect this self, which was constantly searching for the meaning of life, was also Froebel's ideal. His two greatest experiences in life so far had been his knowledge gained from self-education and his love-relationship with Caroline von Holzhausen. Both these experiences, according to Froebel's diary entries, indicated a unity of purpose. To answer the question 'what is man?' one needed to find the underlying 'natural laws', which made this unity explicit. Man, after all, was part of nature and it seemed therefore logical to try and discover 'what is nature?'. To see the unity in nature Froebel enrolled to study physics, chemistry and mineralogy. Froebel's diary entries tell us that the notion of unity occupied his thinking already during the fateful last months in the Holzhausen family. Only when male and female ideas fertilised each other's thinking could clarity of recognition take place. Only marriage could provide such spiritual and mental powers, only such love provide knowledge about oneself. It was the unifying factor which led to the recognition of truth. These realizations came to Froebel when walking alone through the starlit nights of August 1811, while searching for peace and understanding. It was the basis of his 'spherical laws' which he now developed in Göttingen and without which his Kindergarten system with all its advantages and limitations cannot be explained.

What does Froebel mean by the spherical law? Froebel takes as his starting point the 'self' - the self in its totality, that is - it is eternal, unique and complete in itself. Such a self, because it has its existence here on earth, must express itself. It has to take on form and shape and does so through its actions, which take place in the environment in which it exists, that is within nature. These actions and activities emanate from within, from the centre, 'spherically in all directions, just like the heavenly bodies in the cosmos'.[8]

Froebel speaks of an illuminating insight, experienced during his time in Göttingen, which provided him with the effectual and penetrating *spherical* view of all aspects of nature and of human life. This represented recognition that the sphere contains all basic laws relating to the universe, the physical, the psychical, the moral, the intellectual, the feeling and the thinking world; a law which demands that objects and events be experienced, viewed and recognized intrinsically, leading to the realization that every phenomena in its essence is unique and yet part of the whole, all emanating from one source and returning to this source; a conviction that the essence, the substance, the reality of things has to be grasped from within.

As every action creates a reaction which Froebel characterises as plus and minus and of equal value, he is subsequently able to introduce the 'law of opposites', which was later to play a major part in his educational thinking.

At this time, however, the spherical law led Froebel to the recognition that however much one action is differentiated from another they will all lead to an 'allsided harmony and unity of life, re-establishing its original unity' of the self. Everything functions in relation to God, the total Unity, yet each self has its own purpose which needs fulfilment here and now. Such fulfilment, however, is only possible when the self recognises itself for what it is. Self-knowledge is only possible in the examination and the recognition of the values of the opposites. To be able to see unity in such duality (or diversity) and to act accordingly provides man with the potential to represent the eternal in his life on earth. Only the self which fulfils his calling achieves perfection.

It is clear that Froebel's ideas of self-fulfilment had little in common with the Romantics' notion of unfettered individualism. Froebel's spherical law recognised the uniqueness of each individual but only in as much as it contributes to the law of nature, which is unity. Just as freedom can only be understood in terms of the restraining factors from which it is free, so individual differentiation can only be seen in terms of the totality to which it contributes. This concept of unity eventually enabled Froebel to create the first Kindergarten 'as the mediator between the home and the school' and to open the first Women's Training College for Teachers in Central Europe 'because we shall never succeed in the educational process unless we also involve the other half of humanity'.

Froebel left the University of Göttingen in 1812 in order to concentrate on the study of crystallography, under Professor Weiss at Berlin University. Recent discoveries of mathematical formulae underlying the formation of minerals seemed to open up, in his view, another field of study worth exploring. Even though Froebel searched for the most eminent professors to attend their lectures, his approach was essentially autodidactic, looking for confirmation of the correctness of his spherical law, rather than detailed knowledge about the structure of rock formations. Froebel, with all his scientific studies, was still trying to find the answer to the most urgent question 'What is Man?' Possibly unknown to himself, and yet quite unmistakably, he was preparing himself for his life's task - 'The Education of Man'.

The Napoleonic Wars interrupted Froebel's studies. Germany, as a State, did not exist. Prussia, Bavaria, Saxony, Holstein and many other little kingdoms and dukedoms were sovereign states with their own little armies and were no match for the well-trained and well-equipped French. Napoleon's march through Central Europe into Russia brought devastation, plunder and murder in its wake. Anger against the invaders, especially among the students and the young people, was growing, but not until the philosopher Fichte's famous 'Address to the German Nation' was this followed with a call for arms. Froebel too followed this call and joined the army at Easter 1813. His unit was never involved in battle and many a night was spent talking around camp fires. His companions were Christian Langethal and Wilhelm Middendorff, both theological students from Berlin University. Like most soldiers in any war, they talked about the things which had gone wrong to produce the situation in which they found themselves and what was needed to prevent it happening again. Froebel's diary indicates that in fact they were discussing philosophical topics like: 'Man's search for the most noble and best'. Their comradeship and friendship, their shared experiences of suffering and hardship among the civilian population, their awakening feelings of a single German nation, all contributed to form an association among these three men which was to last a life-time.

With the restoration of peace in 1814 Froebel returned to Berlin University. On the recommendation of Professor Weiss, Froebel was offered and accepted the position of scientific assistant at the Mineralogical Museum in Berlin and in 1816 was offered the post of curator of the newly opened Mineralogical Museum in Stockholm. During these two years, however, Froebel had come to see more and more clearly that his inner life would never find fulfilment in work with books and stones. Much to the consternation of his superiors, especially Professor Weiss, Froebel was now ready to exchange a financially secure position for the chance to 'live out' his educational ideas (7 September 1816).

This opportunity was provided by the death of his brother Christoph. Christoph, a parson, had given shelter and care to a plague-ridden French soldier and had died after contracting the disease himself. Froebel felt an obligation to act as father to his brother's three young children and moved to the family's home in Griesheim where he started his first educational institution. It is significant that the first lesson recorded took place in the village stream where master and pupils dammed the flow of water in order to work out the effect of erosion.

Within a few days the number of pupils had risen to seven. Froebel's brother Christian had sent him his two sons, Langethal his younger brother, and one other child had also joined. Middendorff arrived within six months and stayed with Froebel as his co-worker all his life until he took over the institution after Froebel's death. When Langethal also joined his two war-time companions, it became clear that new premises had to be found for this growing enterprise.

An old, derelict farm in Keilhau was bought cheaply and by 1817 the institution transferred to this tiny village of twenty houses and ninety inhabitants in the Harz mountains. By 1820, Froebel's brother Christian, his wife and three daughters had joined the institution. The number of pupils grew from 12 in 1820 to 56 in 1825.

The communal life in the institute was simple and spartan. Food consumed was locally grown, and supplemented by the produce of the institute. Tobacco, coffee and tea were foreign luxuries and so were not used. The dress of the boys consisted of short linen trousers and linen shirts, as also was the dress of the men. Boys and men changed into long trousers when the weather demanded. The rules were the same for teachers and children alike. Nothing was demanded of children which the adults were not prepared to do themselves. When children went for their morning run and swam before breakfast, teachers would lead the way.

The two barns needed re-roofing, the house needed new doors, windows and floors. One of the newest building projects needed completing. At the same time the corn in the fields and the steep hills around Keilhau was ripening and demanded attention. Adults and children planned and worked together. All these tasks were undertaken not merely because they were necessary, but because they provided 'schooling' in Froebel's sense of the word. Froebel always insisted that life itself was the most important school for man, and that unless a school was related to life, it had no claim to its name. Living and schooling in that sense were synonymous.

This, of course, did not prevent the community from introducing 'lessons' as such. Middendorff, a most sensitive, gentle and perceptive person, taught classics and poetry and was most popular with the younger children. Langethal, the brilliant theological student who had been offered a promising career after his finals, taught languages, history and German. Froebel, the architect of the institute, in the widest sense, hovered over them all. He provided the inspiration to meet the challenges and made sure that all the different activities made one unifying whole. He did little direct teaching in these early days, but would often present the children with genuine problems and leave the children to solve them in their own ways. 'Once the problem was solved, Froebel appeared, was pleased about the individual solutions, gave new inspiration and departed.'[9] Everything was directed towards making children think. Songs were all composed by the children as well as the teachers. The hills, mountain tops, streams and paths were given new and more appropriate names, many of which are still used by the local population today. Children were asked to design their own wooden building bricks which Froebel had made by the local carpenter and then handed out as Christmas presents. Geographical knowledge was acquired by walking along the river bed from its source to its confluence with a larger river, by sitting on top of a hill and making a map and then comparing their own creations with official maps. Such explorations extended to plants, trees, insects, birds and stones, each studied minutely. Specimen collections were popular among younger and older pupils alike.

On Saturdays, when the yard had been swept by adults and children working together, the floors scrubbed, the gardens tidied, the animals fed and provided with new straw, the pupils would sometimes be given permission to set off on their war-games. Boys and girls would form two equal teams, occupy a hill-top unknown to the other side and the boys then would try to occupy each other's camps during the night. The girls would keep the camp-fires going and fry the sausages. After peace was re-established both sides would join the midnight feast and spend the night with song and talk sustained by mugs of home-brewed ale. It happened that on one such occasion, the pupils did not return until Sunday morning, just in time for Sunday service in the village church. When Froebel looked around him during the service, he found that many of his pupils were fast asleep. Pretending to be worshipping while in fact sleeping was educationally inadmissible. Yet, when Froebel subsequently encouraged his pupils to sleep it off in the hay-ricks on returning from their Saturday outings, he drew upon himself the displeasure of the parson and some of the villagers. This was not the only time that his educational ideas were to bring him into conflict with the church.

*Henriette Wilhelmine Hoffmeister, Froebel's first wife who supported him for almost thirty years. She died in 1839, thirteen years before Froebel.*

Christoph Froebel's widow, who had used the money from the sale of her house in Griesheim to pay for the farm in Keilhau, had done so in hopeful expectation that Friedrich would marry her. Froebel had no such intentions so his sister-in-law, having little interest in Froebel's venture, left Keilhau within a year. The institute was left urgently in need of a head of household. Froebel, who had entertained a lively correspondence with Henriette Wilhelmine Hoffmeister since they first met during his university years in Berlin, now asked her to marry him. There were difficulties. Wilhelmine had been married before to a high official in the Ministry of War, and had obtained a divorce on grounds of ill treatment. She was reluctant to tie herself again in marriage. Her father, an aristocrat, was strongly opposed to the marriage, and there was the added complication that Wilhelmine was most unlikely to have children - as a consequence of her sufferings during her first marriage. None the less Froebel and Wilhelmine were married in 1818.

Considering that Froebel's intellectual and probably also his emotional ties to Caroline von Holzhausen continued until 1831, and considering also that Froebel and Wilhelmine too suffered much because they were denied the joys of parenthood, it was a considerable achievement that the marriage survived until Wilhelmine's death in 1839. Froebel's emotional involvement with his two young nieces produced another shadow over their marriage and also created great anxiety among the Keilhau circle. His fierce struggle with himself during this episode may well have been of a sexual nature, a result, no doubt, of his frustrating experiences with Caroline von Holzhausen.[10] Wilhelmine never criticised and her modest demands, simplicity of life-style and her readiness to serve Froebel and his cause made her an ideal partner. Froebel honoured and respected her and gave her the position to which, as his wife, she was entitled. The marriage grew in strength and harmony as the years went by, reaching a truly equal and mutually supportive level during the last eight years of Wilhelmine's life, when she worked with Froebel on the Gifts for the first Kindergarten.

It was probably inevitable that several of the young people in Keilhau should find their marriage partners from within the community. When Wilhelmine's first marriage broke up, she took a foster daughter into her home who accompanied her to Keilhau. Ernestine Crispini grew into an intelligent and cheerful young woman, and married Langethal in 1826. Froebel's other war-time comrade and co-worker Middendorff also married into the Froebel family in the same year. Froebel's older brother, Christian Ludwig, had been living with his family in Keilhau since 1820, partly because he did not want to be separated from his sons who had joined the Institute from its very beginning, and partly because he had sold his own home in order to support his younger brother's venture. He had three daughters, and Middendorff married the eldest, Albertine. The second of the three girls eventually married Barop, the youngest of the teachers at the time, and the man who eventually took over the Institute after Froebel and Middendorff had died.

Within these close ties, people strove to live a life in harmony and unity, where financial gains counted for little and poverty and debts were accepted as part of their everyday lives. Yet they never lost their belief in serving a higher goal: the education of man. This was the climate in which boys and girls grew up and which found expression in the school inspector's report: 'What the children know, they have seen from within and demands expression of inner necessity.'

While Germany was celebrating the tercentenary of Martin Luther's Reformation by setting up stone monuments, the Keilhau community created a 'living monument' when they searched for, found and accepted into their institute two of Luther's descendants. These two boys were living with their parents in poverty, herding swine and cattle. The older of the two eventually went to university to study theology while the other became a stonemason and after Froebel's death carved his grave-stone in the shape of the first Gift.

Swimming, sledging, games, running and walking were part of a well-planned programme, which also included activities for the good of the community: levelling the sportsfield, building a road, extending houses and bringing in the harvest. Festivals were celebrated with song and dance and the stillness of the night consciously experienced by sitting together under a starlit sky. Many of the experiences were the same for young and old alike; adults called themselves with the familiar German *Du* , accepting the same constraints and enjoying the same freedom as their young charges. Yet even amid this equality Froebel seems to have stood out as somebody different. Julius Froebel, his nephew and pupil wrote in his later life:

> Friedrich Froebel was one of the most remarkable men of his time. The head, with its parted hair falling down to his shoulders, appeared priest-like. His profile was most regular, almost classical; the expression sharp and puritanical. When, as a child, I saw him for the first time, he appeared to me different from all other men, and in the Institute he was almost considered to be a higher being. His gift as an educator was extraordinary and in other times among other men he might have become the founder of a religious order. His inspirations to think of and provide interesting activities for young people of any age were inexhaustible. Idleness and slackness were therefore not known in the Institute, even the most spoilt young men who were brought to us, as to an educational Spa, from time to time, were soon affected by the spirit of a strong, fresh and active life and quickly forgot their bad habits through the constant activity of mind and body .

How unfortunate then that growing numbers of pupils led to the employment of teachers who were not able to commit themselves fully to the aims of the institute. Dr Herzog and the teacher Michaelis succeeded particularly in creating unrest among pupils and staff. Froebel probably reacted too vehemently against these dissenters, but the disunity created by the staff in Pestalozzi's school was still fresh in his mind. Both teachers soon left the institute, and although Michaelis and Froebel parted without animosity, Michaelis managed to persuade Julius Froebel, for whom the institute was founded in the first place, to leave Keilhau in 1825 and to follow him to Munich.

Julius studied in Munich, became a Member of Parliament in Frankfurt, wrote a book on *Social Politics* and was eventually denounced as an atheist and a radical. His brother Karl, also now opposed Froebel, but completed his education at Keilhau before leaving. Froebel never took these dissensions personally, but saw in them a limited understanding of the community's basic aim: 'the renewal of life born in the spirit of the education of man'.

Criticisms of a different kind were levelled against Froebel and the community from Government circles. Ever since the German States had achieved freedom from Napoleonic rule and oppression there had been unrest in the country. The young men who had returned from the war against the French felt that such dark days of occupation should never again become a reality. German unity was a pre-condition for achieving this. The demand for a united Germany was strong (especially among German students). The Austrian and Prussian Governments were agreed on a common policy of strong measures against the rebels. One of these measures was also to affect Froebel's educational institute.

The institute had become suspect because of its revolutionary approach to education. Pupils were given much more freedom of choice than in any other existing school in Germany at that time. Teachers and pupils wore the same dress, an Old German costume, and boys and men let their hair grow long. The Prussian Government ordered an investigation and, in September 1824 and again in November of the same year, an Inspector of Schools arrived and took careful note of what he observed at Keilhau. Here are some extracts from this report by Inspector Zeh:

> Both the days which I passed at the institute in the closest intimacy were in every way agreeable to me, highly interesting and instructive, and have raised and strengthened my respect for the institute as a whole, as well as for its director who carried it on and upheld it amid stress of want and care with rare persistence and with the purest and the most unselfish zeal. It was very delightful to feel the influence which proceeds from the fresh, vigorous, free and yet orderly spirit which pervades this institution both in and out of lesson time . . . .

> With great respect and hearty affection all turn to the principal; the little five year-old children cling to his knees, while his friends and colleagues hear and honour his advice with the confidence which his insight and experience . . . deserve . . . .

> The love and respect in which the pupils hold all their teachers find expression in an attention and an obedience which renders unnecessary almost all disciplinary severity . . . .

> Instruction begins at the fifth year of a child's life by leading him simply to find himself (get the command of his senses), to distinguish himself from external things and these from one another, to know clearly what he sees in his nearest surroundings, and at the same time to designate it by the right word, to enjoy his first knowledge as the first contribution towards his future intellectual treasure. Self-activity of the mind is the first law of this instruction; therefore the kind of instruction given here does not make the young mind a strong-box into which, as early as possible, all kinds of coinage, such as now current in the world, are stuffed; but slowly continuously,

gradually and always inwardly, that is according to the connection founded on the nature of the human mind, the instruction steadily goes on without any tricks . . .

. . . from the simple to the complex, from the concrete to the abstract, so well adapted to the child and his needs that he goes as readily to his learning as to his play . . . .

The report then refers to the teaching of the classics and how the oldest pupils had read Horace, Plato and Demosthenes and had translated Cornelius Nepos into Greek. It continues:

I could not but be astonished at the progress which had been made and thorough accuracy. . . .

The aim (of the institution) is by no means knowledge and science merely, but free, self-active development of the mind from within; wherefore nothing is added to the pupil from without which does not enlighten the mind itself, strengthen the pupil's power, and add to his joy by enhancing his consciousness of growing power . . . .

The aim is to develop the *whole* man, whose inner being rests between the two poles of true enlightenment and genuine religion . . . .

What the pupils know is not a formless mass, but has shape and life, and is, if at all possible, immediately applied to life; . . . there is not a trace of thoughtless repetition of the words of others, nor vague knowledge, in the pupils great and small. Everything which they take up they must be able to think; and therefore what they cannot think, they do not take up.

These observations, made by an experienced educator who had come to find fault, demonstrate most convincingly how Froebel's theory was working in practice. They also illustrate some important Froebelian principles, namely: that learning succeeds best when undertaken by a searching and self-active mind; that freedom from rote-learning opens the door to understanding; that discipline is a non-issue in a well-conceived educational programme; that freedom for children to explore, choose and question, can result in responsible actions and is not in opposition to order and harmony; that all learning has to start from where the learner is; that a sound knowledge of children is a pre-requisite for successful teaching.

After such a glowing report, the Prussian Government could hardly interfere. Yet the pressure from Berlin continued so that the Inspector finally recommended that the community dress like other people and that they should cut their hair!

Froebel's reflections on his first seven years' experiences in Keilhau appeared in his book *The Education of Man* (1826). The basic idea that God is the creator and originator of all things and of all life, and that therefore God must also be the origin and goal of man's education, is the guiding light which illuminates all sections of the book. The first part provides the philosophical basis, followed by sections on Man as a child, Man as a boy, Man as a pupil. Thus the concept of a school is defined, and home and school are linked not only in determining what ought to be taught, but so that school is viewed in relation to life generally. Each human being has something of the Divine within him and it is his life's task to develop this. The educator can at first only observe; he must wait and reflect on what the child demonstrates. It is most important to observe older children in their work and younger children in their play, for those actions will indicate children's strengths and inclinations. These will be the educator's guide in his demands and prescriptions without harming the uniqueness of each of his pupils.

The following year, 1827, almost proved fatal for the community. The Prussian Government had decreed that children had to be educated in their own state schools. Accusations of a political nature against the community also contributed to the withdrawal of children. While the institute housed and educated over 60 pupils in 1826, the numbers were down to five by 1829. Because of the growing numbers in the early 1820s, new buildings had been added and old buildings had been extended. The community was heavily in debt at a time when they could least afford it. Yet, builders and craftsmen refrained from taking Froebel to court on the grounds that they would rather lose their money than attack the honour of such a man in court.

It was part of Froebel's character to demonstrate the utmost confidence in the ultimate success of his ideas at a time when collapse seemed inevitable. At this stage in his life he planned for an all-inclusive educational institute where people would be educated from babyhood to adulthood. It became known as the Helba Plan. This plan was Froebel's response to the Duke of Meiningen's request for ideas for the establishment of a school in the Manor of Helba, near Meiningen. Fundamental to the Helba Plan was the idea that pupils had to be educated according to their gifts and abilities. All would start off in the same institution where basic learning was to be achieved through free activity and creative work. There was to be no segregation by either social class, ability or race. Children from Jewish parents were to be admitted in order to overcome racial segregation, which was common in Germany at the time. After attending this first institution children were then to be educated either in 'The German Institute for Art and Crafts' leading to the 'University of Self-Education' or in 'The German Institute for General Knowledge' (Keilhau) leading to the universities as generally known. The Helba Plan also included the idea of a 'Developmental Institute' for pre-school-age children, aged between three and seven. This plan of 1828 is the first time that Froebel considered an institute for very young children. He was at pains to explain that this was not a school, 'for children will not be schooled in this institute, but will develop freely, so that human beings who are no Angels yet, have the possibility to have nurtured and protected that which is divine in man'. Children for this institution would come from the middle classes who had lost their mothers or parents, but who had the means to pay. Though Froebel worked all his life to integrate children from different classes, as documented in the official report on Keilhau by the Inspectorate, he had to establish such a proviso for economic reasons.

Froebel outlines in the Helba Plan his belief that the acquisition of knowledge is the unification of the interaction between life and individual activity, between doing and thinking, representation and cognition, ability and understanding. All the

*Wilhelm Middendorff, a most sensitive, gentle and perceptive person taught classics and poetry and was popular with the younger children.*

education in these diverse institutions should therefore be based on individual activity and self-representation. The 'doing' together with the 'thinking' was to be elevated to an educational aid, and thus physical work was to be seen as part of education. In practice it meant that apart from the pupil's shared responsibilities for the maintenance of the institute (buildings, gardens and livestock) and the planting and harvesting of food produced, the curriculum also included craftwork using paper, cardboard, wood, metal and clay. Many of the items made were utilitarian objects, but the aesthetic quality of the product was to be stressed.

Jealous advisers at the Court of Meiningen made sure that the plan was not brought into operation in spite of the Duke's earlier enthusiasm for Froebel's educational ideas. The Duke's offer to start off with a small school of about 20 pupils was rejected by Froebel. Froebel was so discouraged by the developing mistrust exhibited by the Court that he broke off all negotiations.

In 1828 Keilhau acquired an enthusiastic new teacher, Barop. Intelligent, diligent and well able to deal with anxious parents, Barop soon took over the external leadership of the institute, improving its image and eventually its financial position. Froebel, only too glad to leave these matters to others, was continually driven to find ways and means of spreading his ideas as widely as possible. He left Keilhau to lecture in West Germany and eventually found his way back to the Holzhausen family. Here he lectured to a circle of interested well-wishers, among them a Swiss nobleman of considerable wealth, Herr Schnyder of Wartensee. Schnyder offered Froebel his castle, Schloss Wartensee, to establish his new educational institute and Froebel accepted. Without returning to Keilhau, he journeyed to his new venture in Switzerland.

To explain such a rash and far-reaching decision, one has to be aware of several other events which affected Froebel's life at the time. Froebel had left Keilhau partly because of the financial crisis in the Keilhau community which could well do without having to feed another mouth, especially one which talked incessantly about ideals and showed no interest in the basic practicalities essential for survival. But above all Froebel moved from Keilhau because he was losing his niece Emilie to young Barop. Emilie had been Froebel's favourite niece and for some time had been in his confidence about future plans. His friends and his wife were taking second place. Probably neither Emilie nor the community in general ever suspected how deeply Froebel felt for her. Even though Froebel encouraged the relationship between Barop and Emilie, when it came to the wedding, Froebel had a legitimate excuse not to attend by accepting Schnyder's offer to go to Switzerland. The two letters, which Froebel wrote to the bride and groom on that occasion give us a glimpse into Froebel's inner feelings. The other event which probably contributed to Froebel's quick acceptance of Schnyder's offer may be found in the final break which occurred between Caroline von Holzhausen and himself while staying in their home. Though distance and time had played their part in cooling the deeply felt affection for his trusted friend, not until now did he realize that their spiritual unity was no longer a reality. A new life in a new community might heal the wounds of so many personal losses.

Dark forests, grey rocks, green valleys and snow-covered mountains surrounded Schloss Wartensee, which faced the Sempach Lake. Such abundance of natural variety was equally matched in human terms where German, French, Italian and English-speaking families would provide the pupils for Froebel's new venture. But no sooner had the school opened than an anonymous article appeared in the local press slandering Froebel's integrity by referring to the financial difficulties of the mother institute and implying that Froebel had been forced to leave Keilhau by his staff because of his tyrannical behaviour. Froebel intended to ignore this attack on his person but Schnyder, who had also been insulted in the article, insisted on a public defence. The Keilhau community provided written support without reservation and Froebel came out of the affray without loss of confidence from the local community and the authorities. This event may not have harmed the new institute, but it certainly did not help. There were too few boarders, and not many day pupils as lack of transport to the isolated Schloss presented a major obstacle. The building itself also needed adaptation and Schnyder was not prepared to allow any alteration. Financial difficulties also became apparent and in 1832 Froebel asked for support from the mother institute. The Keilhau community still considered Froebel their spiritual leader and without hesitation responded by sending one of their most able men, young Barop, to join him.

Although numbers of pupils had not increased substantially by the time Barop arrived, the school had a good reputation. So much so that the citizens of nearby Willisau asked Froebel to transfer his school into their little town. As possibilities for extending their work in Wartensee were minimal, Froebel and Barop agreed. Barop undertook the protracted negotiations with the authorities and especially with representatives of the Roman Catholic church who were not pleased by the prospect of a new school under the guidance of a Protestant. Froebel, who had been parted from his wife for three years, took this opportunity to return to the Keilhau community and to report on events in Switzerland. On 1 May 1833 he returned to Switzerland with his wife and the new school in Willisau was opened the next day with 36 pupils.

In spite of unfailing support from the authorities, large numbers of the population harassed the staff of the school, incited by the Catholic clergy. Froebel, Barop and many of the other teachers were frequently warned by well-wishers not to go out on a particular day or attend a meeting for fear of physical attack and danger to their lives. When Barop eventually went to the Canton to ask for protection, he was told that the only way he could obtain it was by winning over the people to their cause. It was therefore decided to hold a public examination of the pupils. People from near and far attended. The examination lasted from seven in the morning until seven at night and was concluded with plays, games and gymnastics. The outstanding success of the day resulted in acceptance by the people in spite of continuing opposition from the clergy. Now that the school was well established Barop felt free to leave and he returned to Keilhau in December 1833.

In 1835 the Swiss authorities asked Froebel to extend his educational venture and to take responsibility for the orphanage in Burgdorf. Middendorff was asked to join Froebel and took over the school at Willisau. He stayed there for four years without a break to see his family in Keilhau. The struggle with the local clergy continued unabated and he felt he could not afford to leave his missionary outpost. Langethal and his wife had also joined their friends in Switzerland, and with Froebel, concentrated on the orphanage in Burgdorf. The orphanage was extended to include an elementary school for the children of the town, for Froebel firmly believed that orphans could and should not be separated from the mainstream of children and that both groups would benefit from such education.

In 1833, the Government in Berne had sent Froebel five young men to be trained as teachers. One year later Froebel and Langethal were also providing a course for sixty students intending to teach. The Success of these courses led to a request by the Government to provide in-service training for practising teachers who were given three months leave every two years. The courses were held at Burgdorf (forty course members at a time) and Froebel once more felt that his work was gaining ground. Young as well as experienced teachers impressed him with the openness with which they approached new ideas. Keilhau was beginning to flourish again under the diplomatic guidance of Barop; Willisau increased its popularity under Middendorff and both institutions took and followed the advice of Froebel who was in continuous and close contact with them.

Yet with all these commitments drawing heavily on Froebel's energy and time, he was still in touch with the children in Keilhau. Many of these letters are still preserved in the archives of the Academy of Science in East Berlin. Study of them reveals the immense care which Froebel took to answer each letter individually. The handwriting is immaculate, deliberately more beautifully executed than in letters to friends or authorities. Each letter picks up a point made by the child which Froebel develops in an educational way to promote further learning. His philosophy, that only the best could produce the possibility of the perfect man, is well illustrated in his correspondence with children.

Ideas expressed in the Helba Plan came to the fore once more when Froebel took charge of the orphanage. For the first time in his life, his educational institute included children of pre-school age. The unsolved problem of how to achieve 'development from within' together with his careful observations of these very young children lead him to the realization of the value of play in a child's education. Life itself became manifest when children demonstrated their inner being through speech, song, dance and their simple representations in play.

But what is this play of the little-ones? It is the great drama of life itself, only in its small beginnings. Therefore its high seriousness, which penetrates joy and pleasure and often becomes dominant.[11]

*Langethal, the brilliant theological student who had been offered
a promising career after his finals, taught languages, history and German.*

Froebel's philosophy of the 'unity of life' where man would be able to understand the meaning of his own life within the universe by working with the media and the means which nature provided, occupied his thinking once again. Man had to become aware of nature and its law in such a way that it provided insights into human behaviour which would guide him for the rest of his life. An 'Institution for Self-Education' had to begin with children before they came to school and their correct treatment was to be based on what nature indicated so strongly to the observer's eye - play. From then on, until his dying days, Froebel searched for the means by which the adult could foster the young child's play so as to help him in his development as an 'acting, feeling and thinking' human being. The regular correspondence with Keilhau at that time, illustrates how the Gifts of the Kindergarten developed. Fully occupied with his 'Early Childhood Pedagogics' and believing it to be fundamental to the success of all further education, Froebel came to the conclusion that the development of such a tremendous idea could best be brought to fruition in the mother institute. His co-workers agreed and, leaving Langethal in charge of Burgdorf and Middendorff in Willisau, Froebel returned to Keilhau in the spring of 1836. Neither institution in Switzerland survived for long after Froebel left. Willisau was abandoned in 1839 because of continued interference from the clergy and Middendorff returned to Keilhau. One year later, Langethal separated from his old friends on religious grounds. He was unable any longer to accept Froebel's humanistic Christianity, and left Burgdorf and became headmaster of a girl's school in Berne. Froebel never forgave him for this break, not because of personal disagreement but because of the effect on the unity of the Keilhau community.

There was one further reason why Froebel returned to Keilhau. Wilhelmine, his wife, had been ill for some time and doctors believed that the sharp air in Switzerland contributed to her ailments. She longed for the gentleness of her Thuringian forests. Froebel and Wilhelmine arrived in Keilhau in the spring of 1836, but Barop was not keen for Froebel to stay in the mother institute for long. He was settled in command now, had managed to save the school from economic collapse and was reluctant to meet Froebel's new demands for financial support for his latest venture. In spirit the community was behind Froebel's new ideas, but they were convinced that Keilhau was not the right place for implementing them, if only for the simple reason that there were not enough children of the pre-school age in the village. The small town of Blankenburg, a few miles from Keilhau, provided the answer. Froebel and Wilhelmine moved into a small rented house, a disused powder-mill, just outside Blankenburg. It was an ideal place for the production of the play-materials with which he hoped to stimulate children to self-education: wooden bricks and balls, prisms and cylinders, soft balls made from wool, cut-outs made from cardboard and wooden frames for weaving. These materials came eventually to be known as Froebel's Gifts and Occupations, which were to play such an important part in the life of a Kindergarten. However, Froebel also needed a press on which to print explanations and instructions for the use of the Gifts.

He created an industrial enterprise, named it 'The Institute for the fostering of the creative activity drive' and employed the most skilled joiners and printers to be found in the neighbourhood. If craftsmen were to work in a meaningful way, they had to be given instruction in the use of the material they produced, they had to know about the aims and purposes of this undertaking and they had to live and work in such a way that this community, though primarily one of production, was also educative and formed a living and growing unit. Froebel took charge of these weekly orientation sessions himself, while singing lessons were given by one of the teachers from Keilhau.

Whenever teachers and pupils from Keilhau went on their travels they would carry in the rucksacks some of these small boxes filled with wooden bricks. Langethal introduced the new ways of playing with children in Switzerland, Froebel's friend and admirer Leonhardi in Frankfurt and the Keilhau teacher Frankenberg in Dresden. Enthusiastic teachers and parents in several parts of Germany were taking up Froebel's challenge to see for themselves that playing with children produced a double reaction: well-being in the child and knowledge in the adult. Froebel recognised that adults who took a child's play seriously and shared this activity with him established human contact at a level where educative growth was part of this interaction and was mutual.

> Play truly recognised and rightly fostered, unites the germinating life of the child attentively with the ripe life of experiences of the adult and thus fosters the one through the other.

While it was more evident that the child would learn from such contact with the adult, it was equally true, though less obvious, that the adult would learn from the child. Not only because the adult would observe a child's interest, inclinations, strengths, and weaknesses, thus indicating to the adult how to proceed in his dealing with the child, but also because he would learn from such observations what the adult once knew but had now been blurred by life's demands, namely the impact of new experiences on children when perceived by a mind free from preconceptions and stereotypes.

Parents and teachers had to be made aware of these ideas and for this purpose Froebel wrote and published a weekly Sunday paper, *Sonntagsblatt*, under the banner 'Come, let us live with our children' (1838-1840). Taken as a whole, these articles provide philosophical and psychological justification for his play-theory and give instructions on how to use the play activities with the children. In these early publications Froebel's instructions are often pedantically detailed and in opposition to what he advocates in general. The notion that the 'Inner has to be made Outer', that adults have to help to bring to fruition what is inherent in the child, is often in stark contrast to the activities amounting to 'exercises' which he prescribes. The traditional ways of teaching are too well established, even in Froebel, to overthrow them all at once. Such inconsistencies are the result of a searching mind rather than superficial thinking.

By far the greatest successes in spreading Froebel's ideas were achieved in Dresden. The Keilhau teacher Frankenberg had succeeded in obtaining the support of the mathematics teacher of the Dresden Gymnasium, Dr Peters. Dr Peters had young children of his own and was impressed with the ease with which Frankenberg gained the children's confidence by playing with them, resulting in interesting conversations, especially with two of his children who were usually reluctant to communicate. Dr Peters also saw clearly the mathematical potentials of the Gifts and was intrigued to see how such simple apparatus could help to establish mathematical concepts of fractions, area, cubic capacity, and geometry in pre-school-age children when he was not too successful doing the same with teenage boys in the Gymnasium. In spite of the attacks by the clergy and also the teacher training institutions in Dresden, which branded the ideas as 'mysticism' and Froebel as a hopeless idealist, more and more parents and teachers expressed interest.

In the winter months of 1838-9 Froebel made his way to Dresden and obtained permission to lecture in the King's palace, Der Zwinger, to which the public were invited. The Queen attended and her prolonged questions at the end of the lecture indicated her personal interest and support. Without difficulties, enthusiastic parents were given government permission to establish a 'Family Institute' where pre-school-age children could live, learn and be actively involved in their own education. This then was the first Kindergarten in existence, even if it was not called such, as Froebel had not found the name of it yet.

Froebel had been in Dresden for barely ten weeks when the news reached him that Wilhelmine was seriously ill. She had not been well for sometime, but at her request, the Keilhau community had not informed Froebel as she did not want him to interrupt his important work which was at last gathering momentum. Froebel left Dresden without delay. Two months later on 13 May 1838, Wilhelmine died. Though she was never able to bear him children, Froebel referred to her as 'the loyal mother'. She had shared his disappointments and his joys, never interfering, supporting always. Froebel's latest plans especially had her undivided attention. She contributed ideas to discussions and to the *Sonntagsblatt*. When Middendorff visited her on the day she died, she asked about the well-being of the children and the women in Keilhau. Her life was spent in care and concern for others. 'Only when she is no more, does one realize what treasure a true woman is' said Froebel. His loss was such that Froebel ceased the publication of the *Sonntagsblatt* for a year. His friends took him back to Keilhau so that he would not have to live on his own in Blankenburg.

For several months now Froebel had been searching for the right name to give his new venture. He was sure that it should not contain the word 'school' in it, as 'schooling' in the sense of 'putting in' was contrary to the main purpose of such an institution. The fostering of a child's nature implied drawing on it, guarding, tending and cultivating it like a good gardener tending a young plant. The name 'Kindergarten' came to him like 'a revelation' and united so many ideas, principles, and visions in one symbolic word. The first Kindergarten was officially opened on 28 June 1840, the day when Germany celebrated the fourth centenary of the development of the printing press by Gutenberg. To give birth to the Kindergarten on Gutenberg's day was to link two events of outstanding educational magnitude.

Wilhelmine's death also delayed Froebel's newest plans, namely the creation of a 'Play and Occupation Institute' linked with an institute for the training of play-leaders. The idea, to combine the care of children with the training of young people for such care, was first published in local papers in March 1838 but did not materialise until June. Froebel was undecided about the location of such an institute and vacillated between Dresden and Blankenburg but decided on the latter when the city fathers made him an Honorary Citizen of the town.

Two young teachers, sent by the Jewish community in Frankfurt, were Froebel's first trainees. The Duke's mother, Karoline Luise, attended the first sessions as an observer and showed her support by sending another young male teacher to be trained whose fees she paid. 'The House above the Cellar' had been made available to Froebel by the town-council. Visitors, locals and holiday-makers were constant observers of the games, occupations and activities which forty young children carried out under guidance and with the participation of Froebel, Middendorff and their trainees. A long strip of land, in front of the house, became an essential part of the Kindergarten. The plan drawn up by Froebel himself and still in existence, shows that the central area was divided into single plots of about a square yard, one for each child, surrounded by a path and adjoined by similar sized plots for growing flowers, fruit and vegetables. On either side of the central area were playgrounds for the children and overlooking all this, a paved area with benches for 'Visiting Parents and Friends of Children'. While each child was free to arrange his own patch and to grow what interested him, the enclosing beds were communally worked, thus emphasising the uniqueness of the individual as well as his responsibility toward the community in which he lived. Such responsibility towards the community extended to the town in general. When Froebel realized how much children enjoyed pushing the wheelbarrow used for gardening, which was far too large to be handled successfully by such young children, he had forty small wheelbarrows made for the collection of litter. The sight of Froebel leading his cheerful group of children through the town, each pushing a wheelbarrow and picking up litter wherever they went, must have amused and amazed the citizens of Blankenburg. Even though Froebel linked this activity with the 'educating word' by composing the wheelbarrow song which focused on the many different uses of this implement, the Honorary Citizen of the town also earned thereby the ridicule of its burghers. Yet many, especially women, became more and more interested and involved. Mothers with young children joined in and asked for advice and suggestions. Older children having spent the day in school, queued up in the evening to play with the Gifts, but when winter came the institute had to close for lack of heating. The work was carried on in nearby Keilhau, though with reduced numbers of children. In the spring they moved back to Blankenburg and this arrangement continued until 1843.

These last fifteen years of Froebel's life were, no doubt, his most productive and most creative period. The development of the Gifts and the creation of the Kindergarten was now followed by his search for providing an educational aid for mothers whose children were still too young to benefit from the play with the Gifts.

Between 1840 and 1844 Froebel worked on the *Mutter -und Koselieder Buch*, (*The Mother Song Book*), which Froebel himself described as 'the genuinely ripened fruit of my struggles'. There are several reasons why such a claim may well be justified.

Froebel had observed, recorded and collected children's games and songs over a long period. Many of the games which he was using with the children in the Kindergarten in Blankenburg were well known, some had been altered and some were new. Working with two young artists from the Keilhau community, the music teacher Kohl and the art teacher Unger, Froebel was living out one of the book's main purposes, that of *Lebenseinigung*, the living and working together of people in unity, harmony and respect for each other. Unger drew the pictures, Froebel wrote the poems and Kohl set them to music. Many of the poems are not worthy of that description. 'I am not a poet', wrote Froebel in March 1844 to Schnyder in Switzerland, 'I am an educator, according to my nature ... which is the most difficult art of all ... but which will not succeed unless it goes hand in hand with poetry, music and the art of drawing'.

Each page contains a story which is complete in itself. The child is encouraged to express his own experiences and knowledge through actions (finger-games), and the words of the songs extend these experiences by introducing new knowledge. The drawings help to represent the deeper meaning of each story in symbolic form. From focusing the child's attention on his own body and limbs, the journey through the book takes him via mother to the family, the house and the garden, stars, moon and the sun into the larger community of the village and the country. Yet each journey is pedagogically the same; from 'the object (event) to the picture, from the picture to the symbol, from the symbol to the comprehension of the object (event) as an intellectual whole; thus to the development of the concept', according to Froebel's intimations in the book.

Froebel was attacked for taking too little account of the psychological and physiological development of the child by exaggerating the function of symbolism. Would an exercise which teaches a child to open and close a box not be more beneficial to him than the exercise of a hand movement indicating 'how a fish swims'? Just as Froebel did not advocate physical exercises for the development of strength and dexterity alone, but always linked these exercises with an imaginative story, so he suggested that finger-games too could be used to recall events and by their representation strengthen images and thus encourage imagination and creative thinking. Because individual activity, thirst for knowledge, aesthetic appreciation, religious awareness and social endeavours were still undifferentiated in the very young child, Froebel strove to present them in a unified manner in each of the songs and stories in the book. They were not to be used to train isolated functions, but in their totality to demonstrate the move from the concrete to the abstract, from the particular to the general, that is the interconnectedness of all things, 'life-unity'. This was the deep meaning and true value of play.

*The Mother Song Book* completed, Froebel turned his creative mind once more to the role of women in the educational process. Nebulous surmises on this topic are suggested in several of his writings before 1840. In a letter to 'The Women of Blankenburg' (25 December 1839) Froebel tries to win for them the office of education, asking them to form women's associations which would have as their main objective the clarification of ideas relating to the successful development of pre-school-age children. Women would discuss new educational ideas, exchanging information based on the observations of their own children. They should at the same time encourage the training of suitable young women so that more institutions could be established similar to the one then functioning in the town. To provide the best training possible, Froebel created a public company and asked the women of Blankenburg to subscribe for one share each so that a model institution could be formed and training facilities be extended.

When Froebel suggested, for the first time, at a teacher's conference consisting of teachers, headteachers, inspectors, university professors, ministers of education that they would never succeed in the education of children unless 'the other half of humanity' were involved and that therefore training opportunities must be provided for women, the all-male audience drowned the rest of Froebel's speech with laughter and great merriment. One of the professors rose to ask: 'Does Herr Froebel mean we shall eventually have women university professors?' - and the minutes record that the assembly once more erupted in hilarious laughter.

Not yet receiving a great deal of public support for a training institution, Froebel carried on with his lecture tours concentrating on the establishment of Kindergartens and women's associations. Although women's associations were soon in existence in several towns around Blankenburg, the establishment of Kindergartens took much longer. Only seven had been opened by 1847 inspite of Froebel's travels to Frankfurt, Nurmberg, Heidelberg, Stuttgart and Worms. Whenever he was not on tour, he was training Kindergarten teachers in Keilhau. Middendorff had persuaded Froebel to give up his house in Blankenburg in order to save the rent, especially as he was out of town so often. Froebel obliged, but was never really happy in the changed atmosphere of Keilhau. The women of Keilhau especially seem to have been in opposition to Froebel. He, after all, was responsible for the renewed outflow of money, of which there was little enough to feed and clothe the members of the community. They had little time for his new plans, and Froebel was aware of it. There were some exceptions however. Middendorff's daughter, Allwina, joined one of Froebel's training courses and so did Henriette Breyman, a great-niece of Froebel's who, after his death, founded the Pestalozzi-Froebel House in Hamburg. On that same course was a student named Louise Levin, aged 30, who became Froebel's second wife five years later, at Whitsun 1851. Louise came from a well-to-do background and had joined the Keilhau community for idealistic reasons, helping out in the household. Seeing Froebel old, lonely and rejected, she made it her special duty to look after him whenever the ordinary daily tasks were done. Having been without a close relationship with a woman for some time now, a genuine counterpoint which was essential for the ripening of the fruits of his thinking, he took Louise into his confidence, and she, genuinely interested, asked to be trained as a Kindergarten teacher. Mutual respect grew into affection, love and finally marriage.

Froebel's efforts to persuade women to take up the education of young children as a career, continued. In 'An Appeal to German Women' (26 June 1848) he writes: '... for if we men work separately, unaided by you and your sex in some permanent and effective manner, we cannot, with all our efforts, accomplish anything comprehensive and satisfactory, either for separate families, still less for the nation, least of all for mankind at large, though the need is everywhere pressing'.[12]

His advertisements in local papers produced some applicants, but in general it was difficult to persuade the daughters of respectable families to be trained for employment. Events took a turn for the better when Froebel's long standing well-wisher, the Duke of Meiningen, offered him one of his smaller castles, Schloss Marienthal, for the implementation of Froebel's latest idea, the creation of an 'Institute for all-embracing Life-Unity'. Froebel's notion of life-unity had been a guiding principle since his university days in Göttingen, though the concept of it changed throughout the years. Froebel had expressed the idea that 'the world needs the example of an ideal state in miniature' and believed that the basis for such a state was to be found in the caring and respectful relationships between man and man. Froebel intended to create the example of such a small state with his new institution which was to include men and women of all ages, an orphanage, a Kindergarten, a training centre for Kindergarten teachers, which apart from offering theory and practice would also encourage the development of students' artistic abilities through the arts and crafts, a school for boys and girls up to university age and a centre for the further development of educational apparatus for children. In the event it never went beyond the training centre and the Kindergarten.

The first course for Kindergarten teachers started with eight students in the summer of 1849 in nearby Liebenstein. Marienthal was not ready for occupation and the Duke had made available some alternative accommodation. This change, however disappointing at the time, turned out to be of great benefit to the Froebel movement. Liebenstein was a well-known spa, frequented by the aristocracy and the rich. Froebel's uninhibited involvement with the children's play-activities in and around the parks of the spa created a considerable amount of curiosity and amusement among the visitors and earned him the derisive title 'The Fool of Liebenstein!' To watch the tall and lanky old man hopping with his students and the children like a hare, or joining in their circular dances became a daily highlight of the holidaymakers. More sensitive and thoughtful people, however, began to ask questions, among them Frau von Marenholtz-Bülow and Frau Johanna Goldschmidt (née Schwabe), both of whom became enthusiastic disciples of Froebel and worked untiringly for the Kindergarten cause long after Froebel's death. In the spring of 1850, Froebel and his new enterprise moved to the place which was to become his last residence, Schloss Marienthal.

Politically, these were troubled times. The abortive revolution of 1848 in support of greater local autonomy and less interference from state and church had created unrest in many parts of central Europe. Froebel's nephews Julius and Karl were both involved in liberalising activities. Julius Froebel, a sympathiser of the socialist Robert Blum, was drawn into Blum's trial. Karl Froebel, now headmaster of the High School for Women in Hamburg had gone into print about the education of women and expressed leftish and unorthodox ideas. It was this pamphlet which was cited by the Prussian Government, when its 'Verbot' closed all Kindergartens in August 1851.

> As illuminated in Karl Froebel's brochure "Women, High Schools and Kindergartens", the Kindergartens are part of Froebel's socialist system for the education of young people to atheism. Schools etc. which have been created on Froebel's or similar principles can therefore not be tolerated in the Prussian State.[13]

Froebel, who never before had taken up the pen to defend his cause, was now persuaded to write to the King of Prussia. His protestations that his work was in no way connected with that of his former pupil and nephew Karl, and his request for a public inquiry into his person and his work was not a plea for himself, but for the children who once more would be denied that to which they were entitled. Froebel wrote:

> Your Majesty, the matter of childhood cannot belong to a particular party, this is the reason why my work is unprotected by any of the parties. I cannot exclude anyone who is prepared to take what I have to offer, because the children of parents from any party need the right kind of education. But if the Kindergarten idea is rejected by the conservative party, it will follow that the opposition party will come to its defence and thus make it a party issue. Yet, it is never that! . . . Your Majesty, an old man of seventy who does not ask favours for himself, pleads with you in the name of childhood: do not allow the germ of a new education for morality, law and religion to be trampled on. Take it under your all-powerful protection so that it may flourish and contribute to the, so much needed, re-birth of mankind. Do not allow the matter of childhood to become a tool of political parties . . . . Therefore I beg you again: have the theory and the practice of the Kindergarten examined and you will be convinced of its harmlessness if not of its benefits.[14]

A public examination of Froebel's work was never held and the Kindergarten Verbot not rescinded in his life-time. Hope was sustained, however, by two educational conferences Froebel attended during the last year of his life. The first one, which Froebel had called himself in Liebenstein (27-29 September 1851) was attended by educators, parsons, dignitaries of the church and the Minister of State of Weimar, all giving support to Froebel's new education and thus, even by their very attendance, a snub to Berlin. The second conference was held in Gotha, at Whitsun 1852. The usually punctual old man arrived late. The first lecture was in progress and Froebel tried to enter unobtrusively by a side-door. The assembly rose like one man, so we are told, to honour the man who had given his life in the service of children. At last, 'The Fool of Liebenstein' was recognised as the leading educator in the land. The ovation he received left him in no doubt about the future of his cause even when he had gone. Soon after this strenuous journey Froebel fell ill, never to recover. He died on 21 June 1852.

The Kindergarten Verbot may have hastened Froebel's demise, it certainly helped to spread his message. Many of his young teachers, mostly women, now left Germany and went to work abroad. In many parts of Europe, America and Asia Froebel's new education was leading to the examination of old practices. What was new? What was different? To find the answer, we need to take a more detailed look at Froebel's philosophical ideas which provided him with the foundations for his educational ideas. Froebel always maintained that one needed to be clear about one's own beliefs about the nature of man, before one could begin to formulate one's educational aims. What was Froebel's philosophy and how did it shape his educational thinking?

1. Lange, 1862, p.32.
2. ibid, 1863, p.524.
3. ibid, 1863, p.530.
4. ibid, 1862, p.56.
5. ibid, 1862, p.72.
6. Halfter, 1931, p.284.
7. Hoffmann, 1964, p.156.
8. Spranger, 1964, p.16.
9. Kuntze, 1952, p.56.
10. Hoffmann, 1964, p.160. [?]
11. Hanschmann, 1875, p.225.
12. Michaelis & Moore, 1891, p.266.
13. Hoffmann, 1964, p.180.
14. Hoffmann, 1964, p.180.

*Froebel's first school was established in 1817 in Keilhau in the Harz mountains.*

# Chapter 2
# The Origins of Froebel's Philosophical and Educational Ideas

Friedrich Froebel, a natural scientist by education and vocation, started from the basic idea that the development of man is similar to the development of all other organisms on this planet. All development is a matter of mediation between opposites, where nature mediates between God and man, the spirit between man's inner and outer life and the Kindergarten between home and school. Froebel encompasses these ideas in his 'spherical laws' where he explains his belief that as man and nature proceed from the same source, they both must be governed by the same laws. The laws of nature are also the laws of life. There is unity in all things.

This basic notion of 'unity of life' underlies all Froebel's thinking. It is the foundation of his relationship with children, the cornerstone of his educational ideas and the basis from which he developed his play material for the Kindergarten. That this should have been the case is not really surprising when we remember that nineteenth-century German philosophy presented us with a succession of transcendental philosophers like Fichte, Schelling, Hegel and Krause, all of whom professed to solve the riddle of life, to reveal the secret behind the universe and to explain the meaning of human existence. Froebel's attraction to these idealists, no doubt, was grounded in his childhood experiences when he lived 'in and with nature' in the parsonage garden and later strengthened during his forestry-apprenticeship years when he began to search for the laws which governed the wonders he observed in the forests of his homeland.

These philosophers' metaphysical speculations produced a succession of unified systems which interpreted God, nature, life in such a way as to demonstrate, at least to themselves and to their followers, that the nature of reality was finally revealed to the human mind. These idealists, with their trust in the power of speculative philosophy, drew their impetus from Kantian philosophy. True, Immanuel Kant had consistently attacked the claims of the metaphysicians to provide theoretical knowledge of reality, yet he provided metaphysical philosophers with the foundations on which to build.

Kant argued that there is no metaphysical doctrine the truth of which can be verified by experience and that such doctrines could only be established by pure reasoning alone. It may be an understandable desire of rational beings to construct a picture of the universe acceptable to the human mind, but he points out that our actual knowledge about it will always be incomplete. The idea that the universe is the creation of an omnipotent Being, that this Being demands our adoration and support, that man's immortal soul will one day have to give account of its previous existence, are all speculative statements which we cannot support on the basis of our experiences.

In Kant's *Critique of Pure Reason* we find three propositions. The first is that in the course of our ordinary lives we experience events and notice certain features which it is possible to imagine might have been different. This we record in contingent assertions. We know such assertions to be true from our experience. The second is based on the argument that by examining the concepts we use, we are able to state certain propositions that we can see to be true in that their denial would involve conceptual contradictions. There is no need for empirical confirmation. And the third class of propositions is outlined in Kant's phrase 'the conditions of the possibility of experience'. Such propositions, though statements about the world we live in, are really based on how we perceive this world. 'Our knowledge must conform to objects, but it is also true that objects must conform to our knowledge'.[1] Kant insists on the vital distinction between the world as it is in itself and the world as it appears to us.

It is 'the thing in itself' which was taken up by the metaphysical idealists to demonstrate that Kant's philosophy needed to be extended to be complete. To know that things are 'in themselves' unknowable, that their essence is a subject for hypotheses, provided the basis for a definition of the 'unknowable'.

Accordingly, Fichte views the riddle of life as a moral conflict between the ego on the one hand and the absolute ego on the other. The absolute ego, also expressed as 'the infinite practical reason' or 'moral will' posits nature as a tool for moral activity. In Fichte's philosophy the concept of action, of duty and of moral vocation are most prominent. The means to rise above a life of sensual impulses and drives are constantly available to man. Because man is a rational being, his moral choices, based on social duty and mediated by his conscience will attain the freedom he so desires. Ultimately, however, only by his own actions can man attain the complete freedom, a freedom which is even free of social fetters. Fichte's emphasis on the human spirit as the instrument for the realization of an ideal world and his insistence that man must constantly strive towards the attainment of his freedom by his own actions is also part of Froebel's philosophy of education.

Although Schelling, like Fichte, views reality as the unfolding of absolute reason, he gives prominence to the philosophy of arts and to the role of the genius in society. He believes that the key to an understanding of the nature of reality can only be found in aesthetic intuition. Our existence, argues Schelling, is not to be found in the rational conception of God, which, at any rate, can only be apprehended in symbolic form, but in the realization that God is to be conceived as action and as will. As man has the power to choose between good and bad, he is able to sublimate his lower nature and subordinate it to the rational will. Only in his later writings does Schelling postulate man's need for a personal God and occupies himself with man's fall from and return to God.

Hegel, like Fichte and Schelling is concerned with the Absolute, but not in terms of action and will, but in terms of thinking it. He defines the Absolute as Spirit or as the self-evolution of Absolute thought. Hegel therefore places great emphasis on the exploration and understanding of man's spiritual life. He is concerned with expressing the life of the infinite and its relation to the finite in conceptual thought. Law, morality, the arts and poetry are treated as having the same subject matter as philosophy, namely 'absolute spirit', only the specialists have isolated them from the totality of human life.

Froebel's philosophy of education incorporates many of the ideas of the Romantics, especially those about the relationship between God and man and about the philosophy of nature as the mediator between the two, about man's need to be creative and his desire for freedom to achieve this.

Froebel's vision of God as manifest in nature has led many writers to the belief that his religion was not a Christian one, but pantheistic. Yet Froebel himself repeatedly expressed that all his thinking was based on the interpretation of the Christian religion. At the teachers' conference in Rudolstadt, four years before he died, he declared: 'I work so that Christianity may become a reality'.[2] Froebel's concept of the nature of man was essentially a Christian one.

Early childhood experiences had introduced Froebel to the Christian religion. But while his doctrinaire, hardworking and strict father taught him about the God of justice and of righteousness, his considerate and friendly uncle, with whom Froebel lived from the age of ten onwards, introduced him to the God of love. It was his regular discussions with his uncle that brought Froebel to the realization that God was absolute unity and that man strives for this unity; unity with one's own life, unity with one's fellow men and unity with the creator and his creation.

The relationship between man and God was most perfectly demonstrated by Christ. Froebel interprets the uniqueness of Christ by postulating that God used a man who 'absorbed His whole being in himself, and who was therefore His son'.[3] Yet this Christ is not considered to be the means by which man can find his way to God, but a supreme example of the unique position which man occupies in creation. At the same time it is also an outstanding example of an ideal relationship between a father and a son, a relationship which is worth our careful consideration so that we may emulate it.

Froebel does not make any reference to the cross nor the resurrection. Christ may be an example to follow but he was neither an example of power nor of domination. But then this 'power' was not needed in Froebel's philosophy, for man was essentially good and not crippled by original sin as in certain manifestations of the Christian religion.

Even though Froebel's treatment of the Christian religion was selective, focusing on the perfect and the beautiful so as not to spoil the ideal, his central theme was constant and consistent. Man is a member of a larger whole, a part of something bigger than himself; and this bigger something, this Absolute, must be constantly referred to, if the educator is not to lose his way. The Absolute was permanent and at the same time indicated the direction man had to follow to become perfect.

As God is good, and man was created in his image, it follows that man is good. Of course, Froebel knew from his own childhood experience and from his own observations of other children that they can be stubborn, wilful, greedy, hurtful, but this was because of inappropriate treatment they had received. Evil does not originate in the child, it is the product of a neglectful environment. Yet, Froebel's theory of opposites did not include the reality of evil as the condition of goodness.

Man and nature embody the principle of the divine and their sole task is to bring this to fulfilment. But it is man alone who can achieve consciousness and knowledge of his divinity and through his self-determination attain unity with God. Man could only achieve this by his continuous growth and development where maturity at each stage is necessary for progression to the following stage.

In God's world, just because it is God's, something is steadily expressed, and it is an unbroken progressive development in all things.[4]

Yet man is a member of a family, a community, a nation and mankind and his growth can only be harmonious in relation to these larger units. The goal of every man is to attain unity and harmony within himself, with nature and the people around him, and finally with himself and God. This is achieved in two ways which are ongoing throughout man's life. On the one hand, man must become conscious of the truth of the eternal laws as found in nature and adhere to their prescribed boundaries. On the other hand man must embody in outward form the principle of unity and divinity which is constantly demanding expression. Man must create.

Froebel emphasised creative play and indeed the constructive arts because he perceived in the creative activities something divine, as God himself is primarily a creator. 'In order to understand the creator, man must be in a position to create after him, man must himself be a creator.'[5] At the same time man must constantly assimilate the outside world, search for the unity which is there but needs recognition, and seek God in nature through knowledge.

Each individual is unique, has the power to express himself in his distinctive way, yet is subject to a common law, the divine law of unity. It follows that each person has to contribute to the whole in a unique way. Each person, each child has a particular gift which will become visible if circumstances are right and freedom for expression of the same is given. Yet, was it correct to speak of 'giving' freedom when 'working' for it seemed the only safe way to obtain it?

For Rousseau, in *Emile*, freedom was the absence of fetters, whether political, religious or social. Emile has to receive his education in isolation as social habits are, in Rousseau's opinion detrimental to a child's upbringing. Yet in his political writings, especially in *The Social Contract* he exhorts his fellow citizen to preserve the constitution, for only by obeying the law will the individual become free.

Freedom to Kant and Fichte was an independence which was capable of giving a veto to one's own senses and the desires growing out of them. Though man may not yet be free, he has the capacity to achieve this progressively. These ideas were supportive of Froebel's philosophy, though his starting point was somewhat different.

Given that man was the manifestation of the divine spirit in human form, it followed that the divine law was within every human being. It was the task of the will to unfold the law and externalise it. And though the will may be a divine endowment, it is subject to development. Freedom, in Froebel's thinking, is a matter of education. It is the lack of opportunity, within the educational system, for children to make judgements and decisions which produces the adult's lack of ability to use freedom intelligently when he is given it. This, as Nathan Isaacs points out,[6] is one of Froebel's essential principles which, he thinks, is still largely unrealized today.

But whatever final conclusion Froebel reached as regards the nature of God and the nature of man, he maintained from the beginning of his academic career that the answer to these questions must primarily be looked for in the study of nature itself. He reached this conclusion when he was studying at Göttingen. Though at first he included languages as part of his studies, in order to find out more about the growth of intelligence in man, he soon gave this up and concentrated on the study of physics, chemistry and mineralogy because man was part of nature and therefore the first problem to be solved was 'what is nature?'[7]

We have to remember that the one philosopher whom Froebel knew personally and who influenced Froebel probably more than any other, was Krause. Krause was a disciple of Schelling, but also admired Fichte. His contribution to philosophy lay in the attempt to bridge the differing views of Schelling and Fichte.

Fichte, taking his starting point from Kant's *Critique of Judgement*, argued that since life is regarded as a re-conquest by the moral ego of the objective world around us (nature), and since this moral re-conquest implies universal moral order, the moral order was the one true self, the infinite will, the mediator between the self and the spiritual world. To Schelling, nature was more than subjective and more than moral, for him it had an aesthetic unity. Nature was spirit visible and spirit, nature visible. To Froebel too, nature is spirit visible; it intimates spiritual relationships at every point and was, therefore, used by him for the symbolic representation of the spiritual. This is the philosophical basis of Froebel's symbolism which has been so ridiculed by his adversaries. This is easily understandable when we read passages like: 'The ball is the representation of the Universe'[8], or

> Plants are the centre piece of nature because of their similar yet very detailed life cycle. They show men and the child their very own nature by standing in the centre and pointing downwards to matter and particles and upwards to animals and man.[9]

However, there is no need for the educator to go beyond symbolism to mysticism, if he will simply teach nature, not only in its external form, but in its beauty and as a model of comparison with human life in general.

*The playground of Froebel's first Kindergarten in Blankenburg, 1840.
Beds in the centre were the responsibility of individual children. All other beds
were worked and harvested by the whole class.*

The plant's light, warmth, soil, moisture, dew, rain, climate and seasons, are the child's spiritual and intellectual atmosphere, life, philosophy, and actions of his environment.[10]

This is a comparison which facilitates the understanding of nature in terms of 'visible spirit'.

But it would be wrong to believe that Froebel saw nature only with 'spiritual eyes'. Nature to him was also objective and real. It is close at hand and therefore needs our careful study and observation. The garden of the Kindergarten was not only a symbol, it was an essential means for the physical, intellectual, social, and emotional development of the child. Not only were there flowerbeds, herb-beds, vegetable patches, fruit trees and bushes which were planted and tended by all, but each child had his own little plot of land for which he/she was responsible. To learn from the environment around the school was important, yet it was equally important to teach children to care for this environment. This was true of his original school in Keilhau as well as the first Kindergarten which he founded in nearby Blankenburg in 1839.

The Institution will make it its first aim to provide children with an educational introduction to nature, and to encourage observation, but also the care of it - even if only at the level which is appropriate at this stage.[11]

Once the children began reaping the fruits of their labours, Froebel hopefully encouraged the children to use these 'gifts of nature' as presents to others. He once said that there was nothing more beautiful to behold than children's facial expressions when they give voluntarily the product of their labours and care.

Outlining the training programme for Kindergarten teachers, Froebel stipulated that even those who were 'mature and knowledgeable' - and we have to remember, that the entrance qualification for all students was the Teachers' Certificate plus experience in the classroom - would have to attend his institute for at least one year, so that students would be able to 'observe children throughout the four seasons'.

Once weekly 'Nature Walks' were encouraged and eventually became part of the weekly timetable in Keilhau.[12] Teachers were free to concentrate, during these walks, on the subjects they were most suited to teach. Geography, history, German, languages almost any subject could be taught during these walks and 'the study of colours in different seasons and different times of the day' were essential for art work.

But above all, nature provided the strongest evidence possible for the 'unity of all things'. Froebel's first recollection of this idea dates back to his school days, when one of his grammar school masters made him realize that the tree, though complete in itself, is part of a larger whole. It takes from the soil and the air and gives back to both.

In 1811, while taking one of his usual evening walks at Göttingen, Froebel discovered for himself a comet, which during the following weeks excited the learned men of central Europe. Herschel with his advanced telescope calculated that the diameter of the disc was eighty times larger than the earth. Astronomers, philosophers, poets, mathematicians wrote and spoke about it. To Froebel, it gave birth to the law of the sphere. By considering the nature of the sphere, he tried to understand the connection of all things. The sphere has no limits, therefore it unites everything. It presents the manifold in unity and the unity in its diversity. The sphere is the presentation of the origin of all diversity from unity. It is therefore the general as well as the unique and presents the universal as well as the individual, the whole as well as the part.[13]

This, then, is the point of departure from which Froebel endeavours to explain mind, nature, education, life and the absolute. Schelling too argued that nature in its very essence is one. There is one life in all things and one power to be.

Froebel's reflections on the organic connectedness of all things were given a further stimulus by the latest discoveries of Black, Cavendish, and Priestley in England, and Bergmann and Scheele in Sweden. Closer analysis of oxygen, carbonic acid, hydrogen, nitrogen and other gases lead to the organic theory. The limited number of elements (carbon, hydrogen, oxygen, nitrogen, sulphur, halogens and occasionally phosphorus and some metals) employed by nature in building up her vast store of organic compounds seemed to provide scientific evidence for the philosophers that all things were interconnected. French scientists at the same time were discovering the law of chemical equivalence, while Dalton developed the theory of chemical atoms. The universe of Göttingen was full of it and to Froebel it was further proof that he was moving in the right direction.

Froebel probably did not link his reflections on the unity of God and the Christian religion in general with the unity in nature as expressed in the spherical laws until he came across the philosopher Schleiermacher in Berlin. Schleiermacher is mentioned in Froebel's diary entries from 1815 onwards. Froebel was then working under Weiss at Berlin University and had just made friends with Middendorff and Langethal. Both Middendorff and Langethal were pupils and admirers of Schleiermacher's religious-philosophical discourses at the University. Though we have no evidence that Froebel attended these lectures, his diaries show that he knew about Schleiermacher's philosophy and discussed it with his friends on their long evening walks. On 17 May 1816 he recorded:

> Three roads lead the writers of the Bible to the understanding of the truth:
>     through consideration of nature,
>     through the development of the divine in themselves,
>     through observations of inner experiences in relation to them.
> Consideration of nature and man are relative opposites, that is they are complementary. The mind is the unifying factor.[14]

Froebel's diaries (1818-19) show him becoming increasingly occupied with the Christian teaching of the Trinity until about 1820 when he succeeded in identifying his earlier conviction of the unity in nature as expressed in the spherical laws.

There is now a clear shift of emphasis in Froebel's writings after 1820. Until then Froebel tried to formulate his educational principles on the basis of the laws of nature, but in his paper: '*Durchgreifende, dem deutschen Character erschoepfend genuegende Erziehung ist das Grund-und Quellen-Beduerfniss des Deutschen Volkes'*,[15] Froebel outlines the educational ideas underlying his work in Keilhau and starts from religious principles. Religion is the mediating agent between man and God. This agent is active, creative and productive; without it any education would be one-sided and incomplete. Only when he had worked out his philosophy of life and when man had found his proper place in this philosophy did '. . . I feel myself able to turn my thoughts once more to educational problems.'[16]

Froebel's philosophy of education was closely linked to his philosophy of man. Contemporary philosophy of education, on the other hand, though taking account of moral philosophy and epistemology, gives the impression of being primarily concerned with conceptual analysis. Certain educational concepts e.g. 'authority' and 'freedom', 'teaching' and 'learning', 'indoctrination' and 'education' are considered to be important and receive the philosophers' special attention. The choice of these concepts partly reflects the thinking of the society in which we live, partly the preferences of the person undertaking the analysis. This kind of philosophy is concerned with examining the educational practices of our time in terms of meaning and purpose, but in general does not set out to offer any justification for the notions which lie behind the assumptions regarding children's education. Indeed some writers in philosophy of education expressly state that they are not concerned 'with guiding values against which to judge educational provision and educational claims . . . .'[17] but with the *ways* in which people think about educational issues.

Philosophy of education has, of course, not always been treated in this analytical way. By tradition it was normative and system building, outlining aims and purposes of education rather than examining the meaning of words and ideas. Martin Buber for example, links his philosophy of education with his philosophy of the nature of man, and *The Great Didactic*, written by Comenius three and a half centuries ago and conceived as a philosophy of education, opens with an analysis of man's place in the world of which he is the summit.

To appreciate Froebel's own contribution to the field of education demands some knowledge of those educators with whose writings Froebel was said to be familiar. The fact that a great deal of what Froebel accomplished was not completely original, but can be found in the writings and actions of others, does not detract from his achievements. Froebel's original contribution may well be the bringing together of many original ideas to form a coherent whole.

Pestalozzi probably had the greatest influence on Froebel. Froebel records that he went to see him twice in his life time. His first visit in September 1805 lasted for a fortnight, his second visit almost two years 1808-1810. Froebel tells us further that the following writings impressed him greatly: Proschke's *Fragments on Anthropology*, Novalis' works and Ernst Moritz Arndt's pamphlet *Germany and Europe* published in 1805.[18]

The books by Arndt and Novalis laid the foundation of Froebel's philosophy of education, just as Froebel's first experience of teaching in Gruner's school and his subsequent visit to Pestalozzi in 1805 laid the foundation of his methodology of education. Some ideas by Comenius referring to pre-school education were pointed out to Froebel by the philosopher Krause in 1828, and Hanschmann believes that by the time Froebel moved into Keilhau and founded his first school in 1817, he had read Rousseau's *Emile*, the works of the philanthropists and Pestalozzi's writings.[19]

The earliest of these writers who influenced Froebel was Comenius (1592-1670). Comenius believed that man was by nature lacking in goodness but capable of improvement and, like any good bishop of the Christian church, he was convinced of the final victory of goodness in man. In order to succeed, man only needed faith in God, moral integrity and knowledge of the sciences and different languages. The way to bring this about was to be found in nature. Nature provided everything at the right time and in the correct measure and by so doing, it taught man self-discipline and scientific thinking. Just as plants are more easily shaped and formed when they are young, so it is with children. He expressed concern that education was not provided for children below the age of six. He therefore included a 'Mother School' for children aged one to six in his educational system. Yet the subjects to be dealt with in his Mother School were the same as the subjects found in his school for older children. The material to be taught was simply broken down to its most easily understood components and graded in terms of difficulty. We therefore find astronomy, physics, history, politics, geography as part of the curriculum for children in the Mother School.

Comenius' teaching of the same subjects at every age level is considered by Piaget to indicate an 'intuitive grasp of the fact that the same forms of knowledge are essential at each level of development'[20] while Pruefer considers it to be evidence that Comenius, in spite of his great love and concern for young children, did not really comprehend their needs. Pruefer challenges the popular assessment of Comenius as one of the first major contributors to pre-school education and maintains that it is possible to argue that Comenius' influence made later thinking about the education of the pre-school-age child more difficult. He cites in evidence Leibniz (1646-1716), who advocated that Latin, history, and good manners be the subjects to be taught to children up to the age of six.[21]

A comparison between Comenius' *The Great Didactic* and Froebel's philosophy of education demonstrates both similarities and differences. Comenius, like Froebel, drew on nature to illustrate his educational principles, but some of the conclusions drawn from these comparisons differ considerably. Comenius, for example, taught that as the seasons make their appearance in all lands at the same time and cause trees to bear fruit at the same time, so all children must be instructed by the same method and given the same exercises at the same time. Froebel argued that as every plant needs care, attention and nourishment according to its condition, so every child needs individual tuition according to its ability.

Comenius encouraged 'keen rivalry' in the class so that attention was also maintained by those who were not directly involved in a particular exercise, and advocated punishment in cases of inattentiveness and careless work.[22] Froebel discouraged competition on the grounds that children were always trying to do their best anyway and he objected to punishment on the grounds of human dignity, believing also that, as man was born without fault, the cause for unacceptable behaviour was to be looked for outside the child. The action was to be condemned but not the child.

Again, Comenius, like Froebel, suggested that the teaching of reading and writing should go hand in hand, but while Comenius started with the teaching of the alphabet leading to the copying and reading of 'practical information' or to 'instill morality', Froebel started the teaching of reading by referring children to a word they had all used many times before in their own language, a word which was familiar because the concept behind the word was well known. This word was 'Mother'. Froebel seemed to imply that the use of words which were meaningful to the child provided a better foundation for the teaching of reading than the concentration on the teaching of skills. It also fitted into his philosophy of 'unity' which demanded that new knowledge be presented firstly as a whole before one could study its parts. It was essential to focus on the meaning of the word and on the wholeness of the word before asking the child to concentrate on its letters.

Comenius deplored the fact that the teaching of the arts and the sciences was carried out as if they were two completely different entities. Only very few of his contemporaries, he said, had a 'thorough and universal education' for most of them had only some knowledge of either the one or the other. Although Comenius advocated that all teaching be carried out by the same method for all subjects so as not to confuse the pupil, when it came to the teaching of the arts and the sciences he outlined two quite distinct methods. He said that all knowledge in the sciences was gained via the senses:

> . . . the commencement of knowledge must always come from the senses (for the understanding possesses nothing that is not derived from the senses). Surely then, the beginning of knowledge should consist, not in the mere learning the names of things, but in the actual perception of the things themselves.[23]

Comenius therefore advocated that real objects be used for teaching purposes rather than books or words and that if the real objects were not available, at least a model of the real thing could be constructed. The teaching of the arts however was to be based on imitation of the original. Any attempt at imitation had to be as accurate as possible, for although the ultimate aim was 'to accustom the student of art to produce original work', it was 'only practice and nothing else' that produced an artist.[24] Froebel on the other hand put all the emphasis on the learner's active participation, his own activity, as the agent for learning, whether in the sciences or the arts. Imitation too played a large part in his theory, but Froebel's concept of imitation was much wider than the mere notion of copying and included the ideas of re-structuring and re-creation, as outlined in more detail in Chapter Five.

It seems that the ideas that education starts with the day of a child's birth, that subject matter had to be broken down to its most easily understood components and that the principles of education could be gleaned from the laws of nature, represent the extent of the common ground between Froebel and Comenius; there was little else they had in common. There was no mention of the value of play as an agent for learning in Comenius' writings. The only reference he made to play related to the pleasure children experience when building with stones, wood and paper. Because an occupied child is to be preferred to an idle child, play should, therefore, not be discouraged.

Comenius lived and wrote at a time when children were still being treated like miniature adults and anything as frivolous as play was often expressly forbidden, as it 'separated them (children) from God and destroyed their souls'.[25] Not until Rousseau published *Emile* (1762) did educators receive the impetus to re-examine their practices.

The centuries before Rousseau were dominated by civil wars in central Europe. People, fearful of the dangers of chaos created by looting armies, supported strong and law-enforcing governments. But by the time of Rousseau, rational thinking had given way to the Romantics' idealism which encouraged individual liberty, freedom from the shackles of the state and church, and questioned the social order. The granting of freedoms not only referred to the school-child in Rousseau's *Emile*, but also included the infant and the baby.

Rousseau, in his reaction against formal and classical education, preached the escape from the drawing room into the world of nature where man, unspoilt by corrupt society was free to educate his children according to nature and everything surrounding them. Like Comenius, he reacted against 'word-knowledge' and encouraged an active life where children were allowed to run and rush about, to jump and shout if they wanted to. To meet these needs would certainly strengthen their bodies and make them content. Rousseau cites Plato's *Republic*, saying that educators had probably done everything when they had taught their pupils 'to be happy'.[26]

Comenius considered mothers to be ideal persons to educate children from one to six. Rousseau, on the other hand, believed them to be too gentle and therefore placed the education of the pre-school-age child in the hands of the father as soon as the mother had finished nursing. If the father was prevented from fulfilling this obligation then an unpaid tutor had to take on the task.

At the beginning of the educational process, objects with which the child was to be made familiar had to be carefully selected, for unknown objects very often created fear. The emphasis was on learning through the senses, but very soon the child would imitate words used by the adult and, if freedom to speak were not only granted but the child's efforts encouraged, he would soon converse with confidence. Coarse, and even faulty, speech was not nearly as harmful as faltering speech. Rousseau warns against 'verbal learning' and the disadvantages of memorising words without understanding the meaning. The education of children under twelve was to be non-interfering, and the most important rule: to waste time until the child had reached the age when all its faculties had been developed.

It follows from this that the first education should be purely negative. It consists not in teaching virtue and truth, but in preserving the heart from vice and the mind from error. If you could do nothing and let nothing be done, so that your pupil came to the age of twelve strong and healthy but unable to distinguish his right hand from his left, the eyes of his understanding would be open to reason from your very first lessons.[27]

If this created the impression that Emile was free to do as he liked, Rousseau quickly altered this view by pointing out that freedom involved controls and a framework in which it could operate. It had to be a 'well-regulated liberty' where the tutor had the right and obligation to 'control all the circumstances of their pupils' upbringing'.[28] Emile's tutor, though no longer equipped with a birch, is still very much in command, structuring the physical and social environment of his pupil. The greater than customary freedom which Rousseau granted to children was based on his doctrine that children were born 'good' and only contact with man spoilt them.

It was probably the combination of this last idea with his awareness of the dangers of rote-learning that produced Rousseau's thinking on wrong-doing and punishment. Punishment was not to be inflicted by the adult except by putting physical obstacles into the way of the child's indiscreet demands so that the punishment would spring from his own action. Wrong-doing was to be prevented rather than forbidden. This is very much in line with Froebel's thinking, for he advocated that if a child had broken one of the Gifts through carelessness, the Gift should be mended but then returned to the same child for further use, not as a punishment but so that he might be made aware of the consequence of his own actions.

Rousseau formulated, for the first time in educational thinking, Plato's indication that play in its 'natural form' and without interference from the educator had educational value in itself. It educated the senses and it forced the player to make judgements. Play was not only to be tolerated, as outlined by Comenius, but was recognised as an undeniable right of children. There is no indication, however, as in Froebel's writings, that play itself should be used in the service of education, but only the 'natural gladness' in children, the state of happiness, which could be found where children were playing. It embodied the notion that if children were allowed to play and thereby be happy, this happiness would transfer to the learning situation and thus make the pupil more receptive.

Ernst Moritz Arndt (1769-1860) the author of some of the writings which Froebel said influenced him greatly, was born seven years after Rousseau's publication of *Emile*. Arndt is well known in Germany for his patriotic poems written during the Napoleonic wars, but less for a much more important work which Bollnow believes should have secured him a more prominent place in the history of education. It is the paper 'Fragments about the Education of Man' published in 1805, of which Froebel said that 'Whatever noble, whatever excellent thoughts I had about education, I gleaned from this book.'[29] Arndt's picture of contemporary man is that of a shell without a core. He criticised the emphasis on 'all talk and no action' prevailing in his time, man's attempt to explore life in thought only and the artificiality of his reasoning, and like Rousseau, he advised man to return to the source of his existence: nature. He believed that the driving force of man's actions was his instincts and considered these more important than reason. Such instincts were 'natural' drives and children following them could not possibly be evil. To break a child's will in order to make him 'good', as was a common practice in Arndt's time, was indefensible. Original sin had no place in his definition of the nature of man.

In this paper Arndt also talked about stages of development and considered the stage from birth to the age of six of great importance because it was man's most sensitive stage where any contact with him had to be carried out quietly so that the change-over from the child's dream world to reality might be executed gradually. The next stage, from six to fourteen, Arndt characterised by putting the emphasis on the child's demand for an active life which is free from care and fear, and full of wonder and delight. Only in the third stage, from fourteen to twenty-one, did man begin to attain real consciousness and 'pure thought'.

Froebel's educational 'laws of opposites' seem to have been foreshadowed by Arndt's 'polarity of the sexes' where science, knowledge and reason were masculine by nature, and art, imagination, compassion and love feminine. To the child, the father was a symbol of activity and destruction, mother a symbol of creativity and suffering. To explain life in terms of opposites was a basic notion in Romanticism. It led Arndt to another consideration much more far-reaching in psychological terms than anything so far mentioned.

Arndt's belief in the power of instincts as compared to reason transferred the centre of man's actions into the sphere of the subconscious rather than the conscious. Arndt talked in terms of the mixture of 'day and night' which made up man's personality and though the word 'unconscious' was not part of his vocabulary, it laid the foundation for Carus' paper 'Psyche' published in 1846, where the theme was fully developed.

While Rousseau made people aware of the child's right to greater freedom and Arndt indicated a possible supplementary source for learning in addition to the conscious mind, the philanthropists demand our consideration as Froebel's forerunners because of their emphasis on play. Basedow, Salzmann, Campe, Wolke, GutsMuth are probably the most important and among these, the most original contribution concerning the value of play came from GutsMuth.

GutsMuth agreed with Rousseau's idea of the child's right to play, but found the reasons given insufficient. It was not only a matter of the child's right for exercise and relaxation, not only a matter of utilising the 'natural gladness' aspect of play for the purpose of learning, but also a right to a 'fuller life'. For the first time the idea is put forward that work alone is not sufficient to produce a well-integrated being and that the joy and satisfaction found in play are a necessary component of harmonious living. It is an idea which was not really fully developed until the days of the Romantics, an idea which goes well beyond the diagnostic, the recuperative, the exercise, or the learning value of play of Locke. It is the basis of the notion that there is an aesthetic quality in play, a notion which is only now being extensively explored by writers like Buytendijk and Huizinga.

Froebel too was extremely conscious of the aesthetic qualities in life. The suggested activities for which the Gifts could be used, for example, appeared under the headings of Forms of Knowledge, Forms of Life, Forms of Beauty. His pronouncements on language development pay particular attention to the aesthetic qualities of language; and harmonious living for children, in Froebel's opinion, was only achieved when the riches of all three - Knowledge, Beauty and Life (mental, emotional, physical aspects of life) - were all represented in play.

Writers on Froebel who consider the influences of earlier educators on his work invariably mention Pestalozzi. Most writers also refer to the major differences between the two and put lack of cohesion and unity in Pestalozzi's work at the top of the list.[30] This is probably because Froebel himself referred to it in his writings, yet the real differences were much more fundamental and much more far-reaching. The reason Froebel did not enumerate them himself is simply because his own work had scarcely begun when he wrote about Pestalozzi. By the time he had reached his most creative period in life, when his theory and practice were being fully developed, he was no longer concerned with the work of Pestalozzi and rarely mentioned him.

There certainly was disunity among the staff in Yverdon when Froebel was there and, in his opinion, also lack of unity in the subjects taught. Nevertheless, there can be little doubt that Froebel's two years with the great master did affect his thinking about children and their education greatly.

Pestalozzi, like Comenius, Rousseau, and Wolke before him, began the educational process with the child in the cradle. He too, like Wolke, produced a 'Book for Mothers', although *Lienhard und Gertrud*, the simple and moving story of a large family, was probably much more effective in demonstrating the importance of a mother. The *Book for Mothers* though usually attributed to Pestalozzi, was written by his first assistant Kruesi, with Pestalozzi contributing the Introduction and Chapter 7.[31] In *Lienhard und Gertrud* the drawing room became an enlightened classroom and the mother more than a teacher. Comenius' concept of mother as a conscientious teacher is changed by Pestalozzi to the concept of a mother who loves and cares for children without reservation and who knows intuitively what is right for them.

Froebel's picture of the importance of a child's parents is now complete. Froebel's ideal mother cared and loved like Pestalozzi's mother, had to be educated like Wolke's mother, and yet was not sufficient on her own to succeed in the task of educating her child and therefore needed the support of the male in the family, as Rousseau indicated.

Rousseau had condemned contemporary educational methods as 'unnatural' and Pestalozzi took over this idea when he attempted to harmonise his education with nature. It meant that the subjects taught to the child had to be adapted to the ability and nature of the child, and that in general terms one could compare the development of man with that of a plant.

> Man, imitate the action of great nature which from the seed of even the largest tree pushes at first but an imperceptible shoot; but then by a further imperceptible growth which progresses smoothly every hour and every day unfolds the young trunk, and finally the smallest twigs from which will hang the ephemeral leaves.[32]

Pestalozzi's principles that the simple should precede the difficult, that the child's education must match his ability and his comparison of man's development with the growth of a plant, are all concepts found in Froebel's education.

Pestalozzi believed that all knowledge derived from the impressions received through our senses. The mind when faced with new impressions or indeed any situation which needed interpreting, would try to discover three things, namely: how many objects there are in front of the mind (number); their outline and form (shape); and their names (language). Pestalozzi was the first educator to realize that teaching a child was not primarily a matter of imparting knowledge, but a matter of training the faculties needed for understanding.

Yet it was precisely this emphasis on the subjective forms of understanding, on the building up of mental structures, which led Pestalozzi astray in producing meaningless mental exercises which Froebel rejected because to him every action, every thought, every exercise had to have meaning and had to fit - at least symbolically - into the scheme of things. Froebel's objections related to Pestalozzi's methods which reduced learning processes to its smallest components and thus rendered them unintelligible to children. While most of Pestalozzi's teaching started with the parts of a unit, Froebel believed that the whole (or indeed the source of the whole) had to be made conscious before one could look meaningfully at its parts.

> My ambition to become an independent educator and teacher came true at a time when I also had the great fortune to visit Pestalozzi at the height of his creative work in Yverdon. It was during this great educational experience, that I came to the conviction that only an education which comprehends life at its innermost source together with a rounded scientific education can meet the demands of our time.[33]

The comprehension of life at its innermost source could only be achieved by the use of symbols, but symbols which had meaning because they grew out of man's active life and translated his actions back to the inner meaning of life. This indeed is the crucial difference between the two educators. While Pestalozzi, in protest against 'word-knowledge' introduced *Anschauung* (observation of and reflection on the actual object), Froebel introduced the *active*-reflective child.

Pestalozzi's concept of *Anschauung* originated from his conviction that mankind can improve the quality of life only by observing how nature arranged its affairs.

> Lead your child out into nature, teach him on the hill tops and in the valleys . . . .
> Let him be taught by nature.[34]

The example which nature provided was a well-ordered and didactic one in Pestalozzi's eyes. To look at nature and at natural objects carefully, to describe them and may be even reproduce them in some form, was the basis of *Anschauung*. Object preceded words, and peas and stones preceded number. Drawing became important as a means for careful observation, the teaching of geography was initiated by the study of the land on country walks and nature-study by observation of plants and animals on the farm or in the school garden rather than from books.

Pestalozzi's 'object lesson' was the beginning of present day teaching in the physical sciences. The child must be taught to study

> the different conditions of water in repose or in motion, and its transmutation into dew, rain, vapour, steam, hoar-frost, hail etc. then its action and its influence on other objects of nature.[35]

These object lessons were to teach observation and by asking the pupils to describe their observations, also their powers of speech.

Pestalozzi also used the principle of *Anschauung* in his religious and moral education. He objected to the catechism being learnt by heart at a time when children could not possibly understand its meaning and maintained that only a mother's love for the child could demonstrate in an *anschaulichen* way the meaning of the love of God.

Again we detect many similarities between Pestalozzi's ideas and Froebel's writings: emphasis on education based on 'natural laws'; country walks as a basis for the study of geography, plants and animals; objection to teaching religious and moral education by words instead of example.

In Froebel's opinion, however, setting examples, using objects for observations and talking about them was not sufficient for effective learning to take place. Froebel's children not only observed the landscape and drew a map, but followed the stream in the river-bed up to its source and down to the mouth of the river. His children not only observed plants and animals in the school garden, but dug, sowed, planted, reaped, fed animals and looked after them. While Froebel agreed with Pestalozzi in the teaching of moral education as far as Pestalozzi had developed it, Froebel advanced by creating the co-operative classroom where social and moral values could be experienced by children working and playing together.

Froebel believed that the focus which is essential for reflection to take place in young children is not primarily created by *Anschauung*, that is looking and observing, but by the child's self-activity, by his own actions. Only children's manipulation of objects and older children's active representation of what they knew would provide them with the centre of interest which lead to *Anschauung* and then culminated in reflection. Pestalozzi's world of education was that of reflection based on observations, Froebel's that of reflection based on individual activity.

Froebel took a long time to come to this conclusion. The idea that individual activity leads to *Anschauung* was first discussed by Froebel with Middendorff and Langethal in 1817, when they worked out their approach to teaching during daily meetings in their first year in Keilhau.[36] But the notion that individual activity and

*Anschauung* culminate in reflection was not mentioned by Froebel until he was working on the Gifts.[37]

Looking at the educators who preceded Froebel, it will not be difficult to establish links between his ideas about the stages of development in a child, about the 'natural laws in education', about the role and importance of the mother, and even if in a limited way, about the value of play in education and those of his predecessors. But there seems to be at least one educational idea which sets Froebel apart from the others. It is the notion of the creatively active child who has to structure his own learning based on the adult's provision. Neither Rousseau's 'free play' on its own, nor the 'structured play' of the philanthropists on its own could bring this about.

It is this extraordinary combination of Froebel's acquaintance with the writings of men who attributed considerable importance to the education of the pre-school-age child, his partial knowledge of Romantic philosophy which he never studied systematically at university and his very selective treatment of the Christian religion which together produced an educational theory of which play, according to Blochmann[38], became the cornerstone. Froebel's notion of the deeper significance of play could only have come to fruition and been acceptable in the seedbed of Romanticism, and yet, surprisingly, play was not a central issue in Froebel's educational theory at the beginning, but gained importance only slowly, step by step, through his work with and observation of children over many years. How Froebel's ideas of play changed in his life and how these ideas compared with those of other educators is discussed in the next chapter.

1. O'Conner, 1964, p.300.
2. Marenholtz-Bülow, 1876, p.190.
3. Lawrence, 1969, p.172.
4. Seidel, 1895, p.154.
5. Froebel *in* Hanschmann, 1875, p.70.
6. Lawrence, 1969, p.233.
7. Kuntze, 1952, p.43.
8. Seidel, 1883, vol.II, p.40.
9. Froebel, 1842, MS 12/1/8.
10. Froebel, 1838, MS 18/ab 4/F.5.
11. Froebel, 1839, MS 18/8/8a.
12. Froebel, 1840, MS 18/5/1/1-57, p.506.
13. Hanschmann, 1875, p.79.
14. Giel, 1959, p.15.
15. Halfter, 1931, p.562.
16. Michaelis & Moore, 1915, p.89.
17. Thompson, 1972, p.1.
18. Lange, 1862, p.69.
19. Hanschmann, 1875, p.114.
20. Comenius, 1957, p.17.
21. Pruefer, 1927, pp.9-11.
22. Comenius, 1957, pp.67-75.

23. ibid, 1957, p.81.
24. ibid, 1957, pp.87-93.
25. Pruefer, 1911, p.11.
26. ibid, 1911, p.13.
27. Boyd, 1964, p.41.
28. ibid, 1964, p.2.
29. Bollnow, 1967, p.25.
30. Lilley, 1967, p.19.
31. Pruefer, 1911, p.31
32. Pestalozzi *in* Heafford, 1967, p.44.
33. Froebel, 1845, MS 19/8/4 pp.136-7.
34. Pestalozzi *in* Hayward, 1905, p.29.
35. ibid, 1905, p.45.
36. Hanschmann, 1875, p.123.
37. Froebel, MS 8/47/29/94 p.123.
38. Blochmann, 1965, p.3.

# Chapter 3
# How Froebel's Idea of Play Changed in his Life-time and How It Compares with those of Other Educators and Philosophers

Considering that many writers on Froebel believe his 'theory of play' to be the cornerstone of his pedagogy, it is surprising to find that Froebel had little to say on that topic during the first fifty years of his life. Not until about 1836 is his mind really occupied with this concept, and then references to and explanations of the values and aims of play abound.

That team games, as distinct from individual play, had an important function in the education of children became clear to Froebel while he was with Pestalozzi in Yverdon (1808-1810). In his well-known letter to the Duke of Meiningen[1] Froebel refers to the games he played with the Holzhausen children, whose private tutor he was, as follows:

> Bodily exercises were as yet unknown to me in their educational capacity. I was acquainted only with jumping over a cord and with walking on stilts through my own boyish practice therein. As they fell into no relation with our common life, neither with the pursuits and thoughts of my pupils nor with my own we regarded them purely as childish games.

But these 'childish games' when extended to include team games and when properly organised, as in Pestalozzi's school, did become meaningful to Froebel.[2]

> I also studied the boys' play, the whole series of games in the open air and learned to recognise their mighty power to awake and to strengthen the intelligence and the soul as well as the body. In these games and what was connected with them I detected the mainspring of the moral strength which animated the pupils and the young people in the institution. The games, as I now know, formed a mental bath of extraordinary strengthening power, and although the sense of the higher symbolic meaning of games had not yet dawned on me, I was nevertheless able to perceive in each boy genuinely at play a moral strength governing both mind and body which won my esteem.

In Froebel's own school in Keilhau we find games - war-games, dance games, singing games, walking games - as part of the weekly time-table, though on

Wednesday and Saturday afternoons only.[3] They are subordinated to the learning activities and used as a means to create a healthy body which is essential for a healthy mind.[4]

In the *Education of Man* (1826) Froebel devotes less than six pages, out of a total of 335 pages to the importance of play in the child's education. His first reference is to the baby and a warning to parents not to let a child's playing with his limbs become a thoughtless activity and deforming habit. This is followed by the observation that in the next stage (infants) a child's play is 'the representation of his inner life' and therefore most useful to those parents who care to observe it, for it will reveal the 'future inner life' of the man to come. Play for the older child (junior) is referred to mainly as games developing physical skills, strength and courage. There is some reference to symbolic play, but it is mostly descriptive and any interpretation of it is in terms of the child's desire for unity and 'building his own world'. Considering that *The Education of Man* is Froebel's major and best-known work, it is important to realize that what the author had to say about play simply constitutes a reference to the different stages of development and does not even begin to attempt a coherent theory of play.

There is, however, one idea in the last part of the book which merits our special attention.[5] Froebel lists three different types of play. He differentiates between symbolic play, consisting of representations of ordinary life, creative play, where the material used is the only limiting factor, and imitative play, which 'freely recreates' what has been learned in school. He adds that play presupposes an active and purposeful life in and out of school. Such a life will produce rich play which in turn will enhance life. It is the first indication of Froebel's later expanded theory that the structure of play needs to be known by the adult if it is to be used for educational purposes.

In the same year (1826) Froebel also wrote twelve essays and articles dealing with the education of children in *'Die Erziehenden Familien'* (*The Educating Families*), a periodical published by himself. None of these essays has anything to offer as regards play, with the possible exception of a short account of 'Sledging' and the 'Boys' Games in Spring'.[6] In both of these writings the idea is expressed, that a boy's game is really an expression of the total life of man. The boy who walks down to the brook to float his home-made ship, is really approaching the 'fountain of life' and the child who labours with determination up the hill, pulling the sledge behind him, is really like the human spirit who determinedly, unflinchingly and in freedom pursues his established aims. True, it is rarely given to man in later life to pursue his ultimate aim, it is nevertheless present in the spirit of man. But what external life and reality denies, is clearly visible here in the games and play of children. Parents are encouraged to foster these games because of their higher meaning. The symbolic significance of games, of which Froebel spoke in his 'Letter to the Duke of Meiningen', is now beginning to become clear to Froebel for the first time.

It is again taken up in Froebel's *Gundzuege der Menschenerziehung* (*Characteristics of the Education of Man*) written in Willisau in 1830. There we find some references to the importance of festivals (birthdays, holy days, family festivals, youth and community festivals) and the games which are undertaken in connection with these.[7]

> Just like nature's seasons and the changes of day and night . . . so too have man's festivals and games a symbolic meaning. There power is revealed in wisdom while here mankind unites in beauty and joy. As a means of education it demonstrates that play with its free movement can and does illuminate man in his dignity.

In Froebel's plan for the 'School for the Poor' (1833) we detect some shift of emphasis from the symbolic significance of play, to play by which children can learn, though how such learning is to come about is not mentioned. But

> because the child learns easily through play, it must not be left to chance, but has to be an integral part of the curriculum . . . especially physical games.[8]

In 1828 Froebel made personal contact with the philosopher Krause in Göttingen. Long discussions on educational matters took place and we know that Krause acquainted Froebel with Comenius' idea of 'the education of the baby'.[9] Froebel's special interest in the life of the very young child, the baby, can be linked with certainty to this period. In 1826 Froebel published an article entitled 'The Small Child: or the importance of a child's first actions'; in 1830 'The Birth of a Baby' and in 1838 'The Life of the Child: the first actions of a child' and also 'Comparisons: the seedcorn and the child'. But there is at least one other paper illustrating Froebel's concern for the young child's first impressions, first actions and first imitations.

On 6 January 1837, Froebel wrote a paper on 'The New Born Child: The Baby', which, as far as is known, was never published. Froebel outlines the life of the baby and its close link with its mother during the first three months of life. But, Froebel says, something new happens after the first three months have passed. The baby now becomes aware of 'having and not having', of 'past and present', of 'unity and separation'. These first experiences are painful and therefore we, as adults, *change* those new experiences frequently so that the child at one moment 'has a ball and then has not a ball'. We 'play' with the child and play becomes pleasurable.[10]

This is the first time that Froebel turns his attention to play in very early childhood. It is significant too, that he is not satisfied with a mere description, but tries to discover the origin of play at the same time. This observation also reminds us of Piaget's concept of 'the permanence of the object', the establishment of which enables the child to differentiate between self and the rest of the world and at the same time to elaborate his concept of space.

> This progress in the formation of the object is on a par with the correlative elaboration of the spatial field . . . instead of bringing the universe to himself, the child begins to place himself in a universe which is independent of him.[11]

Piaget believes that here we catch for the first time a glimpse of 'the elaboration of the mechanism of intelligence'.

In the same year (1837) Froebel designed his first Gifts. Yet when he produced the first drafts for the use of the Gifts, the ball merely appears as a means to develop individual activity. Play and playing is only mentioned in passing and only in later drafts of the same year is play as such the starting point and the guide line for his play-activities. It is only then, that Froebel and Middendorff worked on the idea together while watching children playing with the Gifts and the concept of play becomes really established in Froebel's theory.

Froebel had now reached a stage in his life which was crucial for his future work. The year was 1837 and Froebel was fifty-five years of age. He had now been teaching for twenty-one years. Play as a means for educating children now became central to his thinking for the first time.

How did this shift of emphasis come about? Froebel left Keilhau in 1833 to follow an invitation to open another school in Willisau. During that time in Switzerland he was also asked to establish an orphanage in Burgdorf (1835). It was this experience with very young children, aged from three to six, which led him to write in a letter to Langethal in April 1835, 'My resolution is quite clear; to devote my life to the fostering of the natural desire for activity.' We notice that the emphasis is still on individual activity.

He left Switzerland in 1836 for Berlin. There he worked further on the idea as a letter to Langethal dated 23 July 1836 illustrates: 'I have made progress, the whole idea is growing', and again on 1 December 1836,

> Since I left Switzerland, I have been at work uninterruptedly, watching over, making clear, developing, shaping and constructing the fundamental idea of my life. I am often, very often quite tired out.

He is referring to the education of pre-school-age children and to the institution which eventually was named the 'Kindergarten', in which play was the central instrument for learning.

For the next seven years Froebel's thinking is taken up with the importance of play as a means of education. During this period he founded the Kindergarten and created the Gifts, the Occupations, the Movement Games and finally probably his most important educational achievement, *The Mother Song-Book* (1844).

The explanations and instructions which accompanied the Gifts, the Occupations and the Movement Games, and which will be discussed in detail later on, provide us with a comprehensive picture of Froebel's continuous re-assessment of the functions of play in a child's life. Froebel finds it especially difficult to work out how much freedom to allow children when they are building with their bricks and how much guidance to provide. While the first version of the explanations to the third Gift, written in 1838, puts the emphasis on 'letting the child play with the bricks and build what he likes', the second version, written six years later, provides mothers and teachers with a blue-print of how to use the Gift and what to build. And yet, one year before Froebel died, the final version is much more like the first version and the emphasis is again on 'freedom in play'.

There are other educationally important concepts which Froebel crystallises in the explanations to the Gifts. For example, he observes that play can only function and develop when the rules and the boundaries in each situation are understood by the player and adhered to. He also makes us aware that a player can only play at and with what he already knows, but that at the same time, the continuation of play depends on the frequent introduction of new materials and new ideas. There will be many occasions when the adult will need to play with the child to give support and maintain interest.

Between 1837 and 1850 Froebel provides us with an abundance of ideas about the educational value of play, but towards the end of his life Froebel turned his attention once more to the symbolic significance of play. It is as if his own emphasis on the intellectual, social and emotional benefits derived from play compelled him once more to underline that play however useful educationally, was more than a mere tool for the educator.

Like Huizinga, he argued that play was essentially a manifestation of the cultural advancement of a society and that the element of freedom was vital for its execution. The notes relating to the preparations as well as the recording of The Children, Youth and Folk Festival at Altenstein in Meiningen on 4 August 1850, which Froebel had organised himself, bear witness to this.

Froebel argues that every period of history, each age, has its own characteristics, just like every season in the year or indeed every time of day. Every human being too lives through certain characteristic stages of development. This is also true of mankind as a whole. But too frequently we live through these periods without being conscious of the importance of our time or the demands which our particular age makes on us. Festivals, such as the one held at Altenstein, (but also family festivals, birthdays etc.,) are the perfect vehicle for making the 'character of our time' conscious.

'Life-Unity' - to live a harmonious life and to grasp the unifying elements leading to it, was the characteristic idea of the time in which Froebel's generation lived. It was therefore important that the Youth and Folk Festival of 1850 be held on a hill with an excellent view over the surrounding countryside, so that people became aware of beauty and harmony and at the same time would realize that they were part of a larger whole. Not only were children and youths to dance, sing and play, but teachers, parents and senior citizens too. They did not only come from Altenstein and Meiningen, but also from, 'Steibach, Schweina, Liebenstein and Marienthal to express Unity.'[12]

It was axiomatic to Froebel that games would start with people forming *circles* and then dancing, moving, and singing within these symbols of perfect unity. Yet people only learn when they also become aware of the 'opposite' of the actions in which they are involved. It therefore becomes imperative that one player be moved into the centre, for the centre point and the circle around it are the visible expression of man's inner and outer life.

The element of freedom is stressed. Children and adults are encouraged to join in, but each one has to partake of his own free will. Only then will happiness and elation result and in turn produce the deeper awareness which is essential in order to understand the close link between the symbolic function of the festival and the reality of life which it intends to interpret.

We have now reached the stage when it may be helpful to compare Froebel's ideas on play with those of other writers. Does the notion of 'freedom in play' produce the same kind of ambivalence as we seem to note in Froebel's thinking?

If we look at the writings of philosophers, psychologists and educators, who have given the topic some serious consideration we find that most of them will consider some, if not all, of the following characteristics as critical to the definition of play. They will say that:

1. Play implies freedom from external and internal demands.
2. Play implies that it takes place within a structured organisation. It is bound by law and order.
3. Play implies a low-level tension between these two, between freedom and order.
4. Play implies the desire for the continuation of that activity rather than the elimination of it through the search for an end-product.

The aspect of freedom in play is mentioned by most writers concerned with the topic. Immanuel Kant considers the 'freedom from purpose' one of the main criteria for play. He says that in contrast to work which one undertakes with another purpose in mind, play is carried out without the intention of such a purpose.[13]

Erikson writes: 'Man must feel . . . free of any fear or hope of serious consequences. He is on vacation from reality.'[14] One could give further examples from Hegel, Herbert Spencer, William Stern etc., who all emphasise that play is free from the demands of the necessities of life, and that it is without consequences. It is not serious, but this does not mean that it cannot be executed in seriousness and with diligence. It is not directed to fulfil a particular purpose, though this does not mean that there cannot be purposeful connections within play.

However, there is a vital difference in the way different writers evaluate this element of freedom in play. To some it is a means which lead to comments like 'we can do as we please', and 'it's only play, you know, we have to remind children'[15] and the evaluative 'only' here stresses the contrast with the objectively serious. It is a judgement which puts play below the serious, below work. Yet there are others who maintain that it is precisely this freedom from necessity which enables man to explore the unknown, to experiment and to create.

W.H. Thorpe in *Learning and Instincts in Animals* writes[16]:

The prolonged childhood of the human species has been of prime importance in freeing appetitive behaviour from the primary needs. This and man's growing mastery of his environment have been the essential first steps not only for play, but for all those activites which transcend mere maintenance and which underlie the mental and spiritual development of man; activities which, though originating in 'play', have produced real advances in knowledge and comprehension of the scheme of things.

Similarly, Bennett in his chapter 'The awakening of the Mind' in his book *The Dramatic Universe*,[17] where he looks at the creative centres of the Dordogne and also South Russia where the majority of the Gravattian 'Venuses' have been found, says:

> The presence of creativity must have resulted in a far greater diversification of behaviour patterns. Life that had hitherto been dominated by food, sex, and self-preservation was complicated by new impulses: intellectual curiosity and the need to understand himself and his world, the urge to express and to fulfil himself, the desire for power and perhaps even possessions, and the need to find new kind of relationships reaching towards a social structure, - these and other characteristic human impulses - must all have entered Homo sapiens' sapiens, with the advent of creativity. The normal outlet for untrained creativity is play.

To these writers at least, the element of freedom in play, the freedom from the necessities of life, from the demands of the self as well as from the demands of others becomes the basis on which the truly human activities of creativeness, discovery, poetry, music and philosophy can be built.

But whatever value we attach to the element of freedom in play, whatever interpretation we accept, the majority of writers on play seem to be agreed that the freedom from external and internal demands is one of the characteristics of play.

Play implies a structured organisation. It is bound by law and order, this was our second criterion. Different writers refer to it in different ways. Buytendijk says that all play takes place 'within certain boundaries'; the Opies talk of the 'confines of a game' which players enter in order to take part or leave and then no longer play. It implies a certain amount of order within the game which every player has to follow.

Again it is interesting to note how different writers evaluate this adherence to the boundaries of play. Dearden, for example, says that play is self-contained in the sense that the rules of games are quite distinct from the rules of the 'serious' as found in law and that play has its special places, time and objects, like nurseries and play-grounds, play periods with a clear start and finish, and its own toys and apparatus.[18]

It is difficult to see what Dearden has in mind when he says that the rules of games are quite distinct from the rules of the 'serious'. The basic rules of any game, whether they be at the level of the adult or the child, are 'to be just'. This is also the aim of the rules which we find embodied in the law of the land.

The other evidence which Dearden offers for the idea that play is self-contained, are the play-spaces, play-grounds, play-periods with a clear start and finish, its toys and apparatus. He cites Huizinga's unique book on play *Homo Ludens* (1951) in support of his argument; the argument that play is something apart from the 'serious' and therefore of a lower order.

Now, the one message which Huizinga repeats over and over again conveys the exact opposite. He says 'To me it is not a matter what place play occupies in a civilization, but in which way the civilization itself manifests all the characteristics of play'.[19] Huizinga puts play in the centre of the 'serious'. True, Huizinga refers to 'boundaries of play' in terms of space and time. But in the example he gives, he not only refers to play-grounds etc. as Dearden does, but also includes temples and law-courts. He refers to these play areas as 'holy ground', apart from the hum-drum of ordinary life, yet influencing it profoundly. But this is not what Dearden has in mind when he says that play is something apart from the serious. He means that it is something apart because it has nothing to do with 'responsible living', 'the serious'.

It is misleading to believe that play does not involve 'commitment' or 'obligation'. A player, for instance, has commitments towards the people who are involved with him in his play. This is true whether a person happens to play an instrument in an orchestra, is a member of a cricket or football team, or whether a young child happens to be playing at 'engines' with his friend. The difference which exists between play and work is not to be found in terms of 'seriousness, commitment and obligation' but in terms of the well defined structures which make play 'self-contained'.

A child, for example, who suddenly disturbs the conversation of his parents by saying 'Look, I am an Engine' will only be able to maintain his play if the response by his parents is that of entering into the spirit of the game and not if their remarks relate back to reality. If the parents say 'Don't make such a noise, granny is asleep', play, at least for a moment will have to cease while the child adjusts to his new situation. But if the parents answer 'Slow down, your passengers are not having a very comfortable ride with all that noise', the child's adjustment can take place within his play. In this particular instance play is circumscribed and enclosed within the world of symbolic representation. It relates back to the idea of being free from the demands of the adult world and at the same time creates its own boundaries.

Play is self-contained in the sense that it can absorb new players and release others, it can expand and retract its activities without changing its forms, shape and structure. One rarely uses the word 'playing' in relation to children who constantly move from one play activity to another precisely because they have not yet discovered the content, structure and boundaries of the activities they are investigating. The second characteristic of play then is its structural organisation with its boundaries well defined and adhered to.

Now, if on the one hand it is true to say that 'play is free' and on the other, that 'play is law-bound', it is not surprising that many writers on play maintain that play is 'ambivalent'. When the writers' usage of the term 'ambivalent' is examined, we find that they are not saying that play is nebulous and uncertain, but that they are referring to a certain tension between freedom and law, between the known and the unknown in play, between the new and the old, which is mentioned as our third characteristic of play.

An awareness of this low-level tension in play is implicit in Froebel's statement that: 'The effectiveness of play is to be found in its constant interaction between law, freedom and life.'[20] Froebel is in fact saying that our first criterion, 'freedom from reality', is only partially correct. The player who plays in complete freedom and in negation of any rules, is soon outside the boundaries of play and finds himself rejected by the other players.

The six year-old in the infant classroom may be free to choose the friends with whom he is going to play and also the objects with which he intends to play, but once he has made his choice, his freedom is restricted, at least to the extend of these two factors. A certain ambiguity has crept into our first criterion, that of freedom, but an ambiguity, an ambivalence, which is a necessary condition for play - i.e. play is rule-governed.

Piaget's definition of play also indicates this kind of ambiguity. To him, play is primarily a matter of repeating that which is familiar. He argues that once we have learned something, once we have accommodated to some new data, we have to repeat it several times in different situations in order to make it really our own; we have to assimilate it to existing schemas. The predominance of assimilation over accommodation is his main criterion for play. He says[21]

> If every act of intelligence is an equilibrium between assimilation and accommo-dation, while imitation is a continuation of accommodation for its own sake, it may be said conversely that play is essentially assimilation, or the primacy of assimila-tion over accommodation.

There must be a tension before equilibrium can be established again. Yet however much repetition of the familiar takes place in play, the familiar is not sufficient to keep play going. Play in any situation, whether we look at adult-play or child-play, has the tendency to extend towards the unfamiliar and towards the more difficult.

The child who first builds a truck with his Meccano, soon strives to build an engine. Here too, then we notice a certain ambiguity, a certain tension between what is known and what is not known, between assimilation and accommodation. Assimilation alone does not seem to be able to maintain play. Play demands a certain low-level tension without which it would die. If this tension on the other hand is so great that it demands the extinction of that tension, play would also cease. This is probably the reason why Piaget is able to say that no schema is completely ludic or non-ludic. There is an element of play and an element of work in everything we do.

Our third criterion then is that play implies a low-level tension between law and freedom, reality and make-believe, the familiar and the new, the predictable and the unpredictable.

As our last criterion we mentioned the characteristic that play implies the desire for the continuation of that activity rather than the elimination of it through the search for an end-product. Writers on play refer to it by saying that 'we play for the satisfaction involved in it', or 'we play for the fun of it'. Now depending on where we believe the emphasis to be, we could get two quite different interpretations. If the emphasis is on 'gaining satisfaction', it could indicate that man has a need to 'play out' ideas and inspirations which may not be granted a proper outlet in the activities of ordinary living. If, on the other hand, the emphasis is placed on 'play for the fun of it', it could indicate a much more fundamental and important criterion for play.

Let us examine both ideas in turn. The notion that play is a matter for 'gaining satisfaction' is probably based on the psychoanalyst's idea of 'tension reduction'. It is argued that all our emotional feelings as well as our actions serve only to eliminate needs and desires. During this process of tension-reduction we experience pleasure. This holds true of play as much as of hunger, sex etc.

All theories of play mention the satisfaction gained from play, but, as Piaget points out, children who symbolically reproduce a painful experience in their play, hardly do so for pleasure. They re-live these experiences not to preserve pain, but in an attempt to understand them, to make them more bearable.

Though Piaget convincingly illustrates that not all play is a matter of 'gaining satisfaction', it certainly is still an example of 'need-reduction'. Yet it is one of the characteristics of play, that once a person is involved in its activity, he desires to go on playing. There is no evidence of an inner compulsion, or drive to eliminate this activity. The psychoanalysts comparison of play with hunger and sex illustrates this clearly. The drive to satisfy hunger culminates in the elimination of that drive through the final act of eating. To satisfy one's drive means to re-establish peace against the existing excitations; one aims for freedom from tension. Play on the other hand does not seek an end-product, but finds fulfilment in the *ongoing* activity. Kant has it:

> In work the occupation is not pleasant in itself, but it is undertaken for the sake of the end in view. In games, on the other hand, the occupation is pleasant in itself without having any other end in view.[22]

Koestler's definition of play points out that the borderline between play and non-play is extremely fluid. He cites two people playing a friendly game of chess in a coffee house one day and being opponents in a tournament arranged by their clubs, the next day. Koestler argues that though the people involved were 'playing' on both occasions, their second involvement was much closer to the demands of the serious than their first activity. He says:

> The degree of 'playfulness' in an action decreases in proportion as the exploratory drive adulterated by other drives, or to put it differently: as the self-arousing and self-rewarding nature of the activity, characteristic of the exploratory drive, yields to striving for specific rewards.[23]

Buytendijk says something similar:

> As soon as a child is utterly absorbed in what he does, be it eating, listening, fetching something, observing, his inclination to play diminishes or ceases altogether.[24]

Yet this is precisely what we observe children doing in many play situations, namely being utterly absorbed, from time to time, in their own activities. At this moment, according to Buytendijk, the child would no longer be playing. Buytendijk seems to suggest that as soon as the child is experiencing something completely new or strange so that the child's whole attention is focused on that new experience, he is adjusting to reality, he is learning. Behind this argument is the assessment that one can only play at, or with, something which one already knows at least in some measure. Froebel too had observed that children only used in their play what they had learned in ordinary life or in school, leading him to the conclusion that the more varied a child's experiences in and outside school, the more creative and intellectually stimulating his play.

In summary, Froebel's early understanding of play was limited to physical games and the way these games facilitated the acquisition of physical skills, strength and courage. This was followed by Froebel's recognition of and differentiation between creative, symbolic and imitative play in which children re-created what they had learned in school or in ordinary life. Froebel observed that the richer a child's life, the richer his play, but it was not until after his observations of the birth of a baby and the baby's first actions and how the adult used these actions to introduce the child to new concepts - concepts like 'having and not having', past, present and future - that he realized the potential of play as a means for education.

The criteria considered to be essential for the definition of play are all made explicit in Froebel's writings, even if only gradually and over many years. The importance and value of freedom in play is mentioned frequently and so is play's dependence on law and order. Froebel encourages parents and teachers to play with their children because he realizes that the continuation of play depends on the interaction between the known and the unknown, between 'law, freedom and life'. Of course, children can keep this low-level tension going on their own, but only when a rich general life provides them with raw materials which they can use in their play. Such play, because of its low-level tension, creates the desire for the continuation of this activity even to the extent that children concentrate so hard that eventually they will fall asleep, as Froebel himself had observed.

No philosopher, no educator before Froebel had seen the importance of play for educational purposes with such clarity. And yet, when Froebel's life drew to a close, he once more emphasised the symbolic meaning of play, believing that a people's culture was play at its most perfect and illuminating. When Froebel said that 'play illuminates man in his dignity', he was echoing Schiller's words that 'only at the level of play is man truly human'[25], for it is the elimination of the demands of the physical and the moral which is the source of man's freedom. And it is the element of freedom in play, as well as education in general, with which Froebel had to come to terms, and which even today is a stumbling block to the understanding of Froebelian education for many. Is it true that in Froebel's schools children were free to do what they liked? What was Froebel's understanding of freedom in education? Why was the Prussian Government so worried about children who asked questions rather than provided answers? Why did Froebel attach so much importance to 'free activity' and 'creative play'? To answer some of these questions, we need to examine the concept of freedom and see what Froebel had to say about it.

1. Michaelis & Moore, 1915, p.74.
2. ibid, 1915, p.82.

3. Lange, 1862, p.360.
4. Froebel, 1831, MS 5/29/13-14.
5. Lange, 1863, p.275.
6. ibid, 1863, p.178, p.353.
7. ibid, 1862, p.442.
8. Froebel *in* Lange, 1862, p.475.
9. Michaelis & Moore, 1915, p.103.
10. Froebel, 1837, MS 18/4/7.
11. Piaget, 1953, p.212.
12. Seidel, 1883, vol. II, p.414.
13. Kant, 1923, p.470.
14. Erikson, 1950, p.185.
15. Peters, 1967, p.84.
16. Thorpe, 1956, p.87.
17. Bennett, 1966, p.251.
18. Peters, 1967, p.84.
19. Huizinga, 1951, p.XVff.
20. Heiland, 1974, p.34.
21. Piaget, 1962, p.87.
22. Kant, 1899, p.68.
23. Koestler, 1964, p.510.
24. Buytendijk, 1933, p.47.
25. Schiller *in* Scheuerl, 1969, p.48.

# Chapter 4
# Freedom and Sensitivity in Education

If we visited a classroom at the turn of the century and then observed the activities of primary school children in their classrooms today, we would probably say that the most striking difference between the two was the level of freedom allowed to our children today as compared with those ninety years ago.

While in the first classroom, children will be sitting in rows of desks, listening to what the teacher has to say and carrying out her instructions, children in the second classroom will probably be sitting in groups or walking about, talking to each other or to the teacher, working on their own or with a friend. Children are free to move about, free to talk, free to work and free not to work. But as soon as we put the last suggestion to our present-day teacher, she will certainly object and say that in her classroom children are not free not to work. This teacher will be expressing some kind of notion that freedom in her classroom is limited. Whatever the limitations, however, there is no doubt that the life of children in schools today is less regulated than it was at the turn of the century.

Such change has by and large been welcomed by parents and teachers alike. Respect for children has grown over the years and with it the conviction that they are capable of making decisions, at their level, which encourages responsibility at a much earlier age than hitherto expected. There were, however, a considerable number of intellectuals, politicians and also parents who considered the new education a dangerous move towards the encouragement of licence and irresponsibility. But while in the past the perennial debate about freedom in education was usually concerned with the treatment of the child in the classroom, it has now moved to the consideration of the freedoms and responsibilities of the teacher. Society no longer believes that teachers can be trusted to carry out their tasks without careful guidance and detailed contracts. Even what to teach and how to teach it is now laid down by law. Central government decides what is good for the child, nation-wide.

Current educational legislation limiting teachers' decision-making in the classroom can be traced back to a philosophy which is fundamentally opposed to the philosophy of the founders of child-centred education. While Froebel believed that children are naturally good and that any evil doing is due to negative influences experienced in later life, the opponents of child-centred education state their convictions as follows:

Children are not naturally good. They need firm, tactful discipline from parents and teachers with clear standards. Too much freedom for children breeds selfishness, vandalism and personal unhappiness.[1]

And if teachers are inclined to emulate the progressives, clearly, means need to be found to stop them from such foolish actions.

Professor Bantock, author of *Freedom and Authority in Education* (1952), is of the opinion that the lowering of standards, which he claims to witness in our present-day schools, can safely be put at the feet of the progressives and especially their masters: Rousseau, Pestalozzi and Froebel.

The pressure on teachers to retrace their steps, to allow less choice, to introduce competition and to stop children from 'playing' is now seemingly unalterable. Yet the philosophies, theories and practices of our greatest educators point in the opposite direction. What are teachers to do and which philosophy should parents support? Let us first of all look at the concept of freedom and then find out what kind of freedom Froebel advocated as a prerequisite for the education of children.

Absolute freedom clearly does not exist; it has meaning only when we use it in relation to something else. When a teacher is saying: 'John is free to paint what he likes', she is simply saying that John is free from any external demands by the teacher to paint something else. When Rousseau advocates a more natural way of living, he mentions at the same time that men ought to be free from the constraints of political institutions and the church. When social reformers desire to improve the living conditions of men, they talk of the freedom from disease, poverty and social injustice. But in all the three examples given, the demand for a freedom *from something* carries with it certain constraints in other directions. The child who is free to paint what he likes is, at this particular moment, not free to read or to play football. Rousseau's advocacy of a more natural life implies constraints by nature in terms of disease, hunger and discomfort. The social reformer's aim to improve the living conditions of men demands the establishment of extensive laws and a system of taxation in order to implement his vision. Clearly, freedom granted or obtained in one area is always counterbalanced by restraints in another area. The same must hold true in the classroom. If we give children a completely free choice of activity in the classroom, it will probably mean that the noise of the woodwork table puts an end to the other children's freedom to choose to read a book.

Froebel too, in his very early teaching career became anxious about the way he taught and became concerned with the freedom from constraint as applied in his classroom:

> Once again I found myself in conflict with my environment; for I could not possibly torture my scholars with what I myself had refused to be tortured with - namely the learning by heart of disconnected rules.[2]

Rote-learning, then, was the first constraint which Froebel recognised as an impediment to education. There seemed to be no difficulty about what to teach, but the way it was done provided concern and disappointment to such an extent, that

Froebel soon left the school in Frankfurt to go to Switzerland to see what Pestalozzi was doing in that respect.

The passage in *The Education of Man*, where Froebel refers to passive education, and which is frequently cited by his critics, gives us the clue to Froebel's second constraint from which he hopes to liberate children. The passage reads, 'Education, instruction and teaching should in the first instance be passive and watchfully following and not dictatorial and interfering.'[3] Froebel goes on to say that only when you have observed a child carefully and when you have determined his abilities can you proceed with the task of education. Froebel here indicates that he wants children to be free from inappropriate teaching; inappropriate in terms of the child's age and ability.

Both these notions of freedom from something, freedom from rote-learning and freedom from inappropriate teaching, led Froebel to a more positive notion of freedom, namely the provision of freedom for children to participate, to choose, to act, to observe, to play and above all to be allowed time to absorb new knowledge at their own speed of learning.

The meaning of positive freedom can best be clarified by turning to Professor Cranston's concise and useful analysis of the concept of freedom. He points out that if we look into the literature of philosophy and politics, we find that the understanding of the concept can be listed under three categories:

1. Freedom as a Faculty.
2. Freedom as Government by Reason (Rational Freedom).
3. Compulsory Rational Freedom.[4]

'Freedom as a faculty' was expressed by Locke, Hume and others who believed that freedom was a power which every person possessed to use as he willed. Man was capable of doing whatever he intended to do.

'Freedom as government by reason' is based on the idea that man is a rational creature, but not wholly so, as he is also subjected to irrational impulses. The ability to choose between these impulses and desires differentiates him from any other creature and constitutes the freedom which has to be realized by a rational assessment of the value of these desires.

Others, like Spinoza and Hegel, have argued that this 'inner freedom' to choose needs frequent support from outside. The mastery of non-rational faculties may have to be enforced in those of limited intellectual ability (like children or the mentally disabled), or when individual interests clash with those of the group. This prescribed, given and directed kind of freedom is 'compulsory rational freedom'. While compulsory rational freedom finds expression in discipline, rational freedom leads to the establishment of self-discipline.

In each case, what Cranston is emphasising is *positive* freedom; freedom is no longer a matter of 'freedom from' constraints, but the gradual freeing of the individual to achieve. Careful observation of children had taught Froebel that even a new-born baby was an active child. The baby's first movements of arms and legs, his first gazes around him and searches were evidence to Froebel that the newly born child was an independent and self-active being. In his observations of 'The Birth of a Baby', probably the only one recorded by an educator of the last century, Froebel comes to the conclusion that not all the baby's behaviour can be considered to be mere reflexes.

> Four to five hours after the birth the child was placed to mother's breast; he sucked heartily and with eyes open . . . .
>
> The inner association of intention to suck appeared already on the first days. For the child brought the fingers to his mouth and opened it in order to suck; at the same time he moved head and arms in a restless manner.
>
> Even in his first hours of life, the eyes turned toward the light and moved in a limited way towards bright objects held before him and remained there; one could detect in these eye-movements a certain amount of attention. Often the child would lie still but look around in a lively manner. - Thus even in the first hours of life we have free-activity.
>
> The little hands held at once tight to an offered finger, but not for long.
>
> The eyes moved in the direction of objects, a blue hyacinth held in front of the child's nose fixed his attention, but not more so than any other bright objects. These exertions seem to tire the child for he yawned several times. - Calmly, attentively and continuously did the eyes search around, coming to rest when attracted by fascinating objects. Here, then, takes place the first education, given by the commonplace situation as it exists. The child needs the (soft) stimulus for his vision and if that were not given, it would weaken and slow down his powers of thinking from the very beginning. But to present the child with such a stimulus for too long would overtax him, just as if the stimulus were too strong. That is true of education at any level which avoids poor learning originating from these two faults (over-stimulation and non-usage).[5]

Of course, the interpretation of Froebel's observations is open to questioning. Can we really talk of 'purposeful looking' in a child's first days of life? Jerome Kegan's research into 'The Determinants of Attention in the Infant', comes to the same conclusion.[6] To Froebel, 'free activity' was observable within the first days of a child's life. Yet he also observed the factors which constrained the child. He observed the lack of control over his movements, he observed the child's limited means of communication, his lack of knowledge. The child was not really free to move in which ever way he liked; he was not even free to control his movements as would seem most suitable for a particular occasion. But his own actions, his independent activity, which would eventually develop into play, could free him from these mental and physical shackles.

Freedom to Froebel was something every child, every man and woman had to attain by his own endeavour. It had to be fought for and involved a conscious struggle towards the ultimate aim which was a life in harmony with oneself and one's surroundings. The following conversation between Froebel and the Minister of Education in Weimar, von Weydenburgh, illustrates this clearly.

> v.W. Do you concur in the axiom of the revolutionists, which is everyone is born free, and brings the right of personal freedom into the world with him?

F.F. No, not in their sense. Man, on the contrary is born fettered on all sides, and truly for this reason, he can and must obtain freedom only by his own striving . . . since it must be the product of our moral and intellectual unfettering, which it is possible to attain only by self-activity. Every individual has to free himself from the narrow fetters of his undeveloped condition of childhood by the help of educational influences . . . . It is the result of consecutive development . . . . The freedom of nations depends on the degree of culture of the majority of their members . . . . The call of the time is the abrogation of the two great differences in culture, the elevation of those unjustly oppressed and neglected.

v.W. Do you mean that diversities in human societies are to be abolished, a levelling and equalising of man to take place?

F.F. Certainly not; for then the manifoldness of human relations would cease upon which depends all equilibrium in this world - the universe in which the infinite variety is the means of order and harmony. But there are two classes of oppressed people: Women and children.[7]

From this it could be concluded that Froebel's concept of freedom is identical to that of 'government by reason' and therefore based on self-discipline. But if we look at the carefully structured play materials which Froebel eventually used with his children, are we not faced with a considerable amount of restriction which might easily be interpreted as falling into the category of 'compulsory rational freedom'? The following discussion based on Froebel's comments about freedom in play indicates that he differentiated between 'free play' and 'structured play' and that even structured play falls into the category of 'rational freedom' because of Froebel's emphasis that its sole purpose is to enable the child to free himself to operate at the level of his own understanding and in accord with his feelings.

A party of prominent visitors, arriving at Marienthal to observe Froebel's 'methods', were surprised about the degree of guidance Froebel exercised during the play activities. One of the visitors observed:

'It seems to me that such continuous guidance on the part of the adult must take away the spontaneity in childish play.'

'A continuous guidance is not practised', said Froebel; 'the children have the larger part of the day to play freely among themselves. Though they are supervised then, it must be done without interference. In the Kindergarten however they are guided in such a manner as to reach the aim desired by nature, that is, to serve their development. Does it disturb the plant in its growth, when the gardener supports it, prunes it, waters it, takes the best care he can of it?'[8]

Here we have evidence to suggest that Froebel, at least at times, seems to prefer 'compulsory rational freedom' for how is 'nature' to be interpreted? Surely it is the teacher's view of what constitutes 'nature' which prevails.

The structuring of a child's play becomes even more obvious when Froebel's Gifts are considered. When, in 1840, Froebel wrote a further, never published, account of the use of the first Gift, the ball, he emphasised that the child will initiate the play with the ball and the educator has to observe the 'free development' of the child according to his ability. But this is only the first step towards the elaborate games which are to follow. The ball is only to be considered as an external means for the child to find himself, to form social relationships to make links with nature, to be active, to consider cause and effect, to draw conclusions and make judgements, to learn colours and numbers, to develop his physical strength, to make words meaningful and to help parents to observe children. Advice and instructions given had to take into account the child's ability. He concludes: 'At any rate, freedom does not include arbitrary actions, nor does it exclude regularity.'[9]

Froebel, then, believed broadly in 'Freedom as government by reason' and though structured play-situations are based on the idea that choices will have to be made for children who are mentally not ready to make them for themselves, as far as we can judge, Froebel did not find this inconsistent with his basic beliefs about freedom. He obviously did not see 'freedom and restraint' as opposites, but restraint as a necessary part of freedom, leading to the freedom to determine one's own actions within the law and demands of the play in which a child was involved.

> . . . he (the child) is free to determine his own actions according to the laws and demands of the play he is involved in, and through and in his play he is able to feel himself to be independent and autonomous.[10]

We have to remember that Froebel was an educator rather than a philosopher. He certainly considered his task to a large extent as one which would persuade people to a more liberal attitude towards children. If mankind was to improve, it could only be done through education and education to him was a matter of 'bringing out' rather than 'putting in'. As man was created in the image of God and God was a free agent, man too was created to be free from external laws and coercion. There were laws to be followed, but these were 'natural laws' to be found in each person. Good education, therefore, was not a matter of establishing laws and pressures from without, but love and self-determination to do right from within. Children, however, had to be helped in this.

Froebel's concept of 'freedom in education' relates to the 'freedom for the child to act according to his ability and inclination'. It is based on the idea that children must be given the right kind of environment and this includes the element of freedom which allows them to see relationships and draw inferences and to make decisions. This concept includes guidance, order and careful planning and does not include arbitrary actions. A truly 'free' person is one who ultimately lives in harmony with himself and with his surroundings and perceives 'the unity of all things'. It comes about through education and everybody has to strive for it himself. Because this kind of freedom cannot be bestowed upon one by others, it cannot be 'compulsory rational freedom'.

In practice it worked like this: An account by Middendorff, Froebel's co-worker at Keilhau, tells of the day when the Gifts which Froebel had designed arrived at his house from the local carpenter. Froebel, his wife and Middendorff were playing with them, when one of the children entered the room. Froebel, eager to try them out at once, called the child over. The child showed no interest in the bricks in spite of encouragement, but focused her attention on some colourful stamps at the end of the table. Froebel's great disappointment was visible, so Middendorff reports, yet Froebel did not press the matter any further, instead he joined the child in her play with the stamps, concentrated on the different colours of these and created some rhyming verses so that the child might remember more easily what she had just learned. Freedom was granted and yet the educator used what the child had to offer for further learning.

> The urge to occupy himself is a child's first expression, as soon as his body and mind begins to develop. This drive increases with his continuous growth and growing strength. The mother, the parents, the teacher are now faced with the difficulty of how to utilise this drive for activity, so as not only to satisfy the immediate needs of the child, but also to plan so that the child's total being is catered for, even as regards his future destiny and demands.[11]

It is possible to accuse Froebel of ambiguity as regards his ideas about 'freedom in education', but there can be no doubt as to what he was aiming for. If play was at times structured to such an extent that it allowed the child little freedom of choice, it was only so that eventually a being might emerge who was able to make his choices on rational grounds. If the choice had to be between a teacher's demands and a child's wishes, Froebel would often consider the child's inclination to be more important, as the above story illustrates. Froebel does not provide us with a blue-print of how to solve the problem, but he has made us aware that the issue when it comes to the education of children is not really one of a dichotomy between 'freedom and authority', but one of when to guide and when to leave alone; a matter of freedom and sensitivity.

How it worked in practice can best be demonstrated by paying particular attention to Froebel's educational innovations created during his most creative period in his life, namely the Gifts, the Movement Games and Occupations and the Mother Songs and examine in more detail the instructions which Froebel provided for the children, parents and teachers. Froebel made it abundantly clear that these were to be taken as guide-lines and recommendations rather than rules to be adhered to. It will also be interesting to note how these recommendations changed over the years. The more he played with the children, the more he learned from them and the more often he needed to update his ideas. Froebel's theory was born in practice.

1. Cox & Boyson, 1975, p.1.
2. Michaelis & Moore, 1886, p.109.
3. Lange, 1863, p.5.
4. Cranston, 1953, p.24.
5. Froebel, 1837, MS 18/4/8.
6. J. Sants & H.J. Butcher, *Developmental Psychology*, Harmondsworth, 1975.
7. Marenholtz-Bülow, nd, p.142.
8. ibid, 1876, p.45.
9. Froebel, 1840, MS 18/5/1/1-57, p.46.
10. Froebel, 1845, MS 19/8/4/136-137f.
11. Froebel, draft for a newspaper article, 1844, MS 19/8/2.

# Chapter 5
# The Gifts

When Froebel focused on the education of pre-school-age children, he realized that children at this age, because they could only progress into intelligent human beings by their own actions, needed to be supplied with materials which would encourage self-activity. This was not merely an exercise in providing toys, but a matter of making available mathematically structured material from which and with which children could learn; material which enabled children to represent that which they knew and that which they understood in parts only; material with which to externalise whatever occupied their minds most and with which to demonstrate those areas in which they were supremely confident and able. They were to be Gifts handed to children, not to signify a present given, but a tool which would help children to indicate their gifts so that the adult would know which areas of a child's interest and understanding to encourage most. For, after all, children learn best by concentrating on that which they know, rather than on that which was still confusing and nebulous. The detailed study of the Gifts not only provides us with information regarding the composition and uses of them, but also introduces us to Froebel's educational principles, applicable to pupils at any age.

The first Gift was a soft ball on a piece of string. Froebel argues that it is an ideal object which even a baby in the cot can handle; it activates the child and to Froebel 'self-activity' is one of the mainsprings of learning. While the child is playing, the ball will be lost and be found again and in this way it will lay the foundation of here and there, of past, present and future, of time and space.

But the ball is also a symbol of unity. No other shape or form is so strong and so complete as the sphere and as it is the educator's task to awaken the higher senses of his being in a child, playing with the ball would also strengthen his inner life. Later editions of the first Gift consisted of six soft balls coloured in the six basic colours derived from the spectrum, namely; red, orange, yellow, green, blue, violet.

The second Gift consisted of a wooden sphere, cube and cylinder. In the first Gift, the child received objects of the same size and shape, but of different colours, thus learning to separate colour from form. In the second Gift, he receives unlike objects and learns to distinguish them from each other by their individual differences of shape and form. The first Gift suggests unity and leads to the discovery of similarities; the second suggests variety and emphasises contrast.

The third Gift had to be something firm, something which a child could easily pull apart and just as easily put together again, because, in Froebel's words: 'All children have the desire to build, and "to build a house" is a universal form of unguided play'. Thus the third Gift is a wooden cube divided once in each direction (height, breadth and thickness) according to the three dimensions which define a solid, producing eight smaller cubes. We move from the undivided to the divided unit, emphasising that unity still exists. The most important characteristics of the gift are contrasts of size resulting in the abstraction of form from size. The idea of relativity is introduced, of the whole in relation to the parts and of the parts in relation to the whole.

The fourth Gift consists of a cube divided once in its height and three times horizontally in its thickness, giving eight bricks. It is like the third Gift in form, size, material and use, but it is unlike in its division. In the third Gift the parts were like each other and like the whole, in the fourth Gift, they are like each other, but unlike the whole. While the parts of the third and fourth Gifts each have six surfaces, eight corners and twelve edges, the faces differ greatly on the new bricks. The increase of difficulty in handling the bricks, necessary for perfect balance, will lead to an increased perception of different dimensions.

The fifth Gift is a cube divided twice in each dimension, providing twenty-seven smaller cubes. Three of these smaller cubes are divided into halves by one diagonal cut, and three others into quarters by two diagonal cuts, crossing each other, making in all thirty-nine pieces. The fifth Gift is an extension of the third Gift, from which it differs mainly because it is divided twice in each direction rather than once, but also because of the introduction of the slanting line and the triangular prism. Triangular forms and the division into thirds, ninths and twenty-sevenths enable illustrations of the plane and cube-root.

The sixth Gift is the last of the solid gifts and is an extension of the fourth Gift from which it differs in size and number of parts. The Gift was indicated by Froebel but developed by his followers and will therefore not be discussed in this chapter. Looking at the instructions which Froebel provided for the use of each of these gifts gives a clear indication of Froebel's ideas of the value of these gifts as well as the value of play in general.

## The First Gift

Froebel published several papers regarding the use of the first Gift. The first draft which circulated among the Keilhau families and later appeared as a series of articles in the *Sonntagsblatt* in 1838, (a periodical published by Froebel from 1838-1840) was published in Wichard Lange *Paedagogik des Kindergarten* in 1861. This first draft will be compared with the final exposition, published in February 1838, issued as a booklet and sold with each Gift. This booklet is long out of print and writers who have since written about Froebel had to rely on the first draft published by Lange. Yet it was Froebel's final version which is by far the more comprehensive and more illuminating of the two.

The first chapter of the first draft provides an exposition of the life of the very young child, how, through his own actions, he expresses his inner life and his self-activity will strengthen his will power. A philosophical argument is put forward to support the use of the ball as the ideal first Gift for the child and this is followed by suggestions of how to use the ball. Froebel then elaborates on several, psychologically important points.

Firstly, Froebel maintains, like Piaget did a hundred years later, that at the beginning of a child's life, the child is unable to differentiate between object and self. He says: 'At first the ball will appear to the child to be one with his hand, like his fist.' This is an advantage, so Froebel says, for the child will hold on to the ball while the playing mother pulls on the string. This will strengthen the child, but this activity will also bring to his notice the idea of 'to have and not to have', of 'unity and separation'.

Next, Froebel points out that it is important to speak to the child while he is playing, and encourages parents to be aware of how they use language, for words emphasise different aspects of our world and therefore have different effects. If we use the words 'tick-tock' while swinging the ball to and fro, we refer to the physical action carried out with the ball. It is descriptive. If we say 'bim-bam', we describe the movement in more aesthetic terms, and when we use 'to-fro', we make a comparison of opposites which appeals to our knowledge and thinking. This quite clearly, says Froebel, links up with the child's physical, emotional and intellectual development.

Finally, Froebel moves from the specific to the general. He says that actions carried out with the ball must now be repeated with other objects, e.g. an apple, a nut, a key, a flower etc.. Because of the different shapes and materials used, the effect of the same actions will be different.

All these activities have to be linked with life as it is. Children will have observed a cat, a dog, horse, chicken, bird, etc.. Children's knowledge is to be used in these games. We can now let the ball 'fly like a bird', 'jump like a cat' and 'bound like a dog'. But also new knowledge can thus be introduced. A squirrel which a child may not yet have encountered, can be described in terms of the characteristics of a cat: fur, jumping, climbing. Parents are not to shrink from introducing material of which the child has no first-hand knowledge. Children are capable of more understanding than we usually expect of them at this age, but parents must be careful not to present such material thoughtlessly, they must not use ideas and objects which are beyond the child's mental grasp.

The final version of the use of the first Gift starts off quite differently. Froebel provides parents and teachers with the reasons for his belief in the value of play. He says that because play consists of a constant interaction between 'law, freedom and

*The first Gift: a soft ball on a piece of string.*
*An ideal object which even a baby in a cot can handle.*
*It activates the child and 'self-activity' is one of the mainsprings of learning.*
*. . . Having and not having, presence and absence, searching and finding, holding, grasping, turning and weighing - all of them leading to consideration of cause and effect, reason and conclusion.*

life', and because play is 'free within certain laws', it becomes a means for self-realization. In play children represent their inner life, that is their knowledge and feelings, and at the same time, it opens up to them the outside world. Play also helps parents to know their children, their aspirations, wishes, strengths and weaknesses.

This is followed by an exposition on the very young child, but the emphasis is shifted from self-activity to unity. Self-activity now becomes a vehicle for 'representation, assimilation and comparison' and because a child makes comparisons in his play, he indicates that he tries to understand the links between things; he desires 'unity'.

Finally, Froebel provides parents with some information about the mathematical properties of the ball and mentions circumference, circle, axis, vertex, opposite angles etc., He says that this is for the parents' own enjoyment, but as Froebel saw mathematical laws underlying all 'natural laws', it formed a fitting conclusion to his latest creation.

When comparing these two papers, we become aware of two basic differences, one relating to the concept of freedom in play, the other to the concept of play itself. While there is no mention of freedom in play in the first draft, it becomes central in the definition of play in the final version. However, it is not just a matter of putting forward the idea that play is 'free' but that it is an interaction between law, freedom and life, involving an alternating process, where both 'freedom' and 'rules' need recognition.

Furthermore, though both papers emphasise the learning aspect, the means by which this is to be achieved are fundamentally different. In the first draft it is the ball which is the means for fostering self-activity. 'The child likes to occupy himself from an early age with the ball . . . in order to educate and develop himself through and with it.'[1]

The word 'play' is mentioned rarely and in passing only. The final version on the other hand starts off: 'Play is the mirror of life' and play becomes the central theme and the means by which the child learns. 'In one word, play truly recognized and truly fostered opens up the world to the child, for which he is to be educated, and develops him for it.'[2] From this time onwards play becomes crucial in Froebel's theory of education.

Froebel considers language to be important because it is part of the environment into which the child is growing and reminds adults that a function of language includes the aesthetic aspect. He emphasises that the first Gift, the ball, though an ideal first object for the child to use, is not an end in itself. It is a means to stimulate interest in life around the child, to make comparisons and to be used for representational purposes - the specific leading to the general and the general leading to the specific. Its diverse uses will create interest and contribute to the continuation of play.

We shall see that from the third Gift onward Froebel grouped the activities to be carried out into 'Forms of Life', 'Forms of Beauty' and 'Forms of Knowledge' and that these correspond according to Froebel to the child's physical, emotional and intellectual development. Such clear-cut divisions are not made in the first Gift, yet Froebel seems to have had them in mind when he devised the exercises.

> The many and diverse exercises will have strengthened the *whole body*, especially *limbs* involved in grasping, holding, throwing . . . . The mind will have been developed . . . for the child had to make comparisons, judgements and draw conclusions . . . . As regards emotional development, his sense of order, beauty, regularity, of the morally acceptable has been nourished.[3]

Though Froebel mentions all three aspects, there is no doubt that the emphasis in both papers is on the child learning. Basic concepts like time and space, correlations between height of fall, speed and force of impact, number and causality, are all involved in these exercises. Movement and their basic configurations like to and fro, up and down, fast and slow, in and out, jumping, rolling, falling, walking, running are stressed, as are concepts which involve relationships between self and object - togetherness and separation, having and not having, presence and absence, searching and finding, holding, grasping, turning and weighing - and all of them leading to consideration of cause and effect, reason and conclusion.

True, says Froebel, these concepts will not all be grasped by the child in the sense in which the adult understands them, and most of these concepts are only used in a very basic and incomplete way, but none of them is false or misleading even in its elementary form.

## The Second Gift - a wooden ball, cylinder and cube

As stated above, the important shift of emphasis from 'self-activity' to 'play as a means for learning' was based on the idea that the interaction between self and the environment leads to comparisons. This idea must have been very much in Froebel's mind when he offered the second Gift to his children - a wooden ball and a cube, with the later additions also including a cylinder as the mediator between the two. It was not only because the child was now older and could handle a hard ball (in comparison with the soft ball of the first Gift), but because the hard ball had certain different characteristics. It is smoother, glides out of one's hand more easily and makes a particular sound when rolled over the table-top and a different sound when rolled over the carpet. It rolls faster and further and can be spun around its own axis. The child cannot help but make comparisons.

Before Froebel continues by giving suggestions of how to use the ball, he explains that in the first instance the child uses moving objects as a means to bring clarity into his incomprehensible world. But it is not movement by itself which lets the child recognise order, but 'repeated movement'. Indeed, it is the rhythm in a child's life which is so important. Therefore, the first game to be carried out with the wooden ball is the rotating ball in a saucer. The idea that we learn by repetition is further developed in the use of the wooden cube. For it is important to repeat some action with different objects and different actions with the same objects. We notice that when Froebel talks of repetition, it includes the element of change, however slight. There is always a comprehensible connection between one event and the next and it has to be made visible. When the wooden cube is introduced to the child, the wooden ball is still on the table. It is difficult to make the ball stand on one spot; Is this true of the cube? - The cube is an object of opposites, that is the reason why the ball and cube belong together. It is not just another and completely new object to play with, but a logical continuation of what went before.

Froebel believed very firmly that 'the law of opposites' applied in the realm of mental development as a whole. We learn by careful observation of opposed concepts and by noticing the differences. Today psychologists talk about 'positive and negative instances in concept formation'. It is when we notice that something which we have hitherto believed to be true is manifestly different or apparently a contradiction, that a new bit of learning takes place. Many of the games of the second Gift are paired to illustrate this. Notice is drawn to the fact that some of our actions will produce an exactly opposite movement in the object used. A cube on a string, hung over a stick, will move up when the string is pulled down and move down when the hand moves up.

The impression of a cylinder is created when the cube is spun around its own axis by two pieces of string, fixed to the cube on opposite corners. Froebel incorporates this into later versions of the second Gift by providing a cylinder, as well as the ball and the cube.

The last two chapters deal with suggestions of how to use the ball and cube for symbolic play and also give advice to parents, again conveying mathematical knowledge as regards the ball, but especially the cube. Educating the parent at the same time as the child was always part of Froebel's theory of play.

Comparing the explanations of the first Gift with those of the second Gift, the idea of 'learning by opposites', indicated in the first Gift, is now elaborated and emphasised. Even repetition has to have the element of change in it, without which interest wanes and learning ceases. A low-level tension between the new and the old, the familiar and the unfamiliar was considered to be one of the characteristics of play.

## The Third Gift - a wooden cube, divided once in each direction to produce eight little cubes

Froebel produced several drafts for the third Gift and at least three different publications are known: Those of 1838, 1844, and 1851. The fact that Froebel occupied himself with this Gift more often than with any of the others - no special publications were produced for the fourth and fifth Gifts except those which appeared in his *Sonntagsblatt*, and no explanations whatever appeared for the sixth Gift - seems to indicate that Froebel attached considerable importance to it.

The first explanation appeared soon after those of the first and second Gifts, in 1838. It was published by Lange in *Froebel's Collected Works* (1862) and it was this version which subsequent writers used and referred to. It demonstrates Froebel's step-by-step thinking about the third Gift. It is not as clearly laid out as the 1844 version, not as complete, yet it is easily understandable, for we are taken through it idea by idea. It has a unity about it, which is based on stories drawn from life rather than the mathematical unity of the second version.

The 1844 version has quite a different atmosphere and emphasis. It is written for the specific purpose of initiating a mother by taking her through all the games which can be played with the third Gift, sometimes with a pedantic accuracy about which hand and which finger to use. The framework of the total picture is introduced at the beginning, leaving the reader to wonder how Froebel arrived at it in the first place. As it is written with the knowledge of six years of play with the Gifts behind it, it takes many things for granted which were available to the reader of the 1838 version. Each play activity suggested is worked out in its final detail and to the last movement, but often without any reasons given.

The 1851 publication is quite clearly produced with the intention of initiating teachers into the play activities. It is almost identical with the 1838 version, but also contains a lengthy addition about the use of the Gift in the Kindergarten when more than one child has to be occupied with it.

One wonders, of course, why Froebel should use the original version of 1838 instead of the more complete and more comprehensive one of 1844. Was he afraid that teachers might adhere to it too slavishly, limiting their own as well as their children's thinking about what they were doing? Or was it that, as plenty of the 1844 versions were available anyway, he wanted to add to the literature by reviving the original version? Or did he believe that the 'unity of all things' and the relationship between the 'inner and outer life' which he so much wanted to demonstrate with all his Gifts, got almost lost in the welter of detailed descriptions and prescriptions of the 1844 version? This is not to say that the 1844 version is of little value. On the contrary, as we shall see, the detailed study leads to statements whose psychological truth has only recently been realized. But if this happened at the expense of 'Unity', was Froebel not compelled to use the original version so as to complete the circle and finish where he had started? We shall never know, but a study of the third Gift will only be complete when we look carefully at all three versions. The original publications of 1838 and 1844 will be used as found in the archives of the Deutsche Akademie der Wissenschaften, East Berlin, and the addition to the final version of 1851, as found in MS 19/12/2/21-26.

The first publication, 1838, is still full of the enthusiasm of these early days when Froebel's ideas about the Gifts found creative expression. He gives a short introductory chapter in which he refers to the signs of the time: young people who no longer respect their elders. Froebel puts forward the contention that the 'old' did not lose contact with young people, but that often they never had it. To provide for a child's material needs is not enough; the child is soon aware of the demands of the heart and mind, and he responds quickly when we do things with him, talk with him and care for his inner life. (By inner life Froebel means a person's thinking, feeling, expectations, desires and perceptions.) The child soon notices when we show genuine concern for him. His inner world, finds expression in his play; if we share his world, we must play with him.

The child at this stage in his development (aged about one to three) strives to separate things, to take them apart, to change their form but also to re-assemble them. The child is intent on discovering inner properties of things and having discovered them, on re-creating the whole. Nothing is more suited to this activity than the cube, subdivided into eight equal-sized smaller cubes.[4]

It is important that the cube be presented as a whole unit first, for the child has to be made aware of the 'wholeness' of things. He will soon take it apart, move the smaller cubes, put them on top of each other and thus begin to build. The watching mother encourages by using words which refer to the child's actions - e.g. up, down, onto - and also by suggesting *what* the child might have built. What kind of objects may such a child represent? We have to remember that a child's paradise is his bedroom, mother's kitchen, father's farmyard. Most probably he will be building a stool, a table, a chair, a bed, a house, a church, a spire. But a chair does not exist in isolation, it might be the chair on which grandmother sits to tell a story. Or grandmother might get up from the chair to fetch the soup from the stove. Where is the stove? - There is the trough. Where are the animals? Where is the shepherd? - The accompanying word is essential not only to describe, but to stimulate recall and perception.[5] Rhymes can be made up and sung as play progresses. A conversation between adult and child may soon follow. No object is to exist in isolation, words will help our imagination to connect them. All these forms and shapes the child has been building are taken from life, we can therefore call them 'Forms of Life'.

But there will be other forms; forms which we cannot recognise as representing particular objects. We may like the forms, we may think that such a form looks like a star, or like an opening flower, but whatever interpretation we may give these forms, they are beautiful. We can call them 'Forms of Beauty'. Froebel then suggested several of such forms, referring the reader to the enclosed illustrations. Every form (shape) must be developed from the previous one. Patterns are constructed which are symmetrical and pleasing to the eye. Cubes are displaced in rotation and each is moved to the same degree. Each change carries within it the change to come, until the series is completed by arriving at the starting position.

There will be forms which are neither recognisable as 'Forms of Life' nor as 'Forms of Beauty'. The cubes may have been arranged in such a way that they constitute two equal parts of the whole. These forms deal with mathematical concepts of the cube, its halves, quarters and eighths and the different ways of dividing fractions. Froebel calls them 'Forms of Knowledge'. Here he puts the emphasis on the conservation of quantity - whatever the shape of the fractions constructed, whichever way they are divided, a half always remains a half. Questions of quantity, volume and size, like number, are closely linked with those of conservation. The basis of correct measurement is the understanding that an

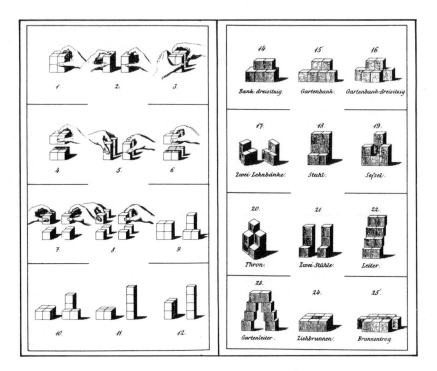

The third Gift: a wooden cube, divided once in each direction to produce eight little cubes.

Forms of Knowledge: An object remains constant in size, volume and quantity whatever its position or arrangement in relation to other objects.

Forms of Life: The child's first representations will be objects encountered in everyday life; a bench, a chair, a ladder.

Forms of Beauty: Cubes are displaced in rotation. Each change carries with it the change to come. Each completed form indicates the new form.

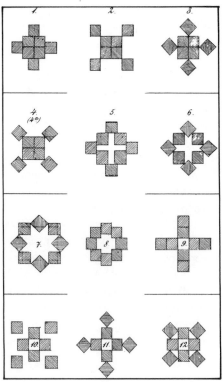

object remains constant in size, volume and quantity whatever its position or arrangement in relation to other things.

Is it possible to use 'Forms of Knowledge' with a three year-old? Froebel believes that in its most elementary forms, it is and he then produces two pages of rhymes which can be used with the actions to explain equal parts and halves.[6]

He concludes his first publication of 1838 by insisting again that though he may be playing with dead objects, language can change this. The purpose of it all is that the child must be surrounded by things alive, not dead. He must perceive life in his play, life's meaning and its harmony.

The second publication of the third Gift appeared in 1844. In the six years between these two publications, Froebel's first venture into pre-school education was moved from Blankenburg to Keilhau because of lack of finance, yet it was also restarted and officially opened as 'The Kindergarten' in Blankenburg. Froebel himself is busy publishing his weekly periodical *Das Sonntagsblatt* (1838 and 1840) for parents, families and all those interested in the education of children. He visits Dresden, lectures to parents and teachers and finds enough support to open the 'Institution for the Care of Little Children' in 1839. Other such institutions in Frankfurt (1839), Rudolstadt (1840), Gera (1841), Barmstadt (1844) follow. Froebel and Middendorff travel widely, lecturing, persuading, inspiring and carrying their message through Germany. They also carry the Gifts with them and demonstrate them with children whenever possible.

It was during that time that an article appeared in the daily paper *Allgemeiner Anzeiger der Deutschen*, of 19 March 1839, written by Froebel. It is headed 'Education. Concerning the Education of pre-school-age children'.[7] It is a short and clear statement of Froebel's thinking regarding pre-school education and as the main purpose of the Gifts is summarised by Froebel, it is worth considering these before turning our attention to the 1844 version of the third Gift. Only the first four paragraphs have been translated.

*Education*

Concerning the Education of pre-school-age children

The longer we consider and examine the present day methods of education, the more clearly we recognise that the children of pre-school-age lack the care and consideration which would be in accord with their present and future needs, *a care which considers equally the child's mental and physical positions.* We notice that if children of pre-school age are not given the care which takes their stage of human development into consideration, they will lack the foundation for the task ahead in school and for their later lives in general.

This realization has accompanied me for a life time, at first nebulous and a surmise only, but I have been increasingly aware of it during thirty years of endeavour in the educational field. Especially during the last years, I have put my ideas for examination before teachers, educators and parents of *all social* classes, whose deliberations, based on their experiences, agreed with mine, *that the present and future living conditions of men of all social classes rest on the careful*

*consideration and the rounded mental and physical care of early childhood, and
that, at the moment, schools and life in general do not possess this genuine and firm
foundation to a large extent.*

This realization, directed my educational endeavours more and more, especially
in the later years, towards the care of children in their earliest years, up to school
age, especially by paying attention to their activity drive, their occupational drive.

Because I find that one of the basic causes of defective childcare is the
unsatisfactory consideration of the children's activity drive, I have endeavoured to
create an institution for this very purpose. An institution under the motto: 'Come
let us live with our children', which has the task of giving into the hands of parents,
families, educators and teachers a coherent system of play activities. These games
do not only nourish the inner activity drive, but they also teach the use of the child's
immediate environment as a means for play and occupation and as educational aids.
They are games and occupations, ways and means, which give a presentiment of the
connection between human life and nature, and an indication of the laws of it, so
as to give an example - at least a symbol - to live up to. Finally, games which are
therefore educative and developing for the person who plays with the children,
which influence him and in their alternating educational function become a genuine
bond between them both.

Realizing how the Gifts were eventually misused by Kindergarten teachers who
followed after Froebel, it is important to consider what Froebel expected the Gifts
to achieve. He envisaged that the Gifts will teach the child to use his environment
as an educational aid; secondly, that they will give the child an indication of the
connection between human life and life in nature; and finally that they will create
a bond between the adult and the child who play with them.

The rest of the article deals with the observation that institutions for pre-school
education will have to be created as parents find it increasingly difficult to occupy
themselves with the children. Six Kindergartens had been opened by 1844, but this
was obviously not sufficient. The training of Kindergarten teachers also made only
slow progress. It was at this stage that Froebel produced a new explanatory booklet
for the third Gift. It is a manual of instructions to a mother, and though 'mother'
includes 'all you who occupy yourselves with the care of early childhood, indeed
with children of any age', there is no doubt that it was primarily directed towards
the natural mother who would have to carry out the task at home because of the lack
of Kindergartens.

'What can I do? - dear father!'

'Dear mother, I know not what I can do!'

are the first two sentences of the 1844 publication for the explanations to the third
Gift. The appeal is immediate and direct. Any philosophical arguments are
supported by examples from the daily life of a mother.

Having persuaded 'mother' to have a closer look at the Gift, Froebel sends her
into her own room and asks her to imagine being alone with a child. She is then asked
to use cubes for building something of her own choice, but whatever it may be, she
should soon give it meaning, name it, and talk about it. When several objects have

been made, it will become quite obvious that certain objects belong to certain categories. One cannot help but compare them, order them, complement classes and groups, and extend them. Even in these early play activities we can observe how the parts create a unit, and how words play an essential part in this.

Once the adult has played in this manner several times, she will observe that any object which has been created falls into one of the following three very broad categories. Objects which are representations of life around us, (Forms of Life), of beauty (Forms of Beauty) and of knowledge (Forms of Knowledge).

Froebel now asks the adult to look at the list of the hundred 'Forms of Life' and to rebuild them. He point out that the order of building them is important, as each form is constructed from the previous one. To destroy one form first in order to create another was educationally unsound, not only because it prevented the child from becoming aware of the 'interconnectedness of all things', but also because it put too much emphasis on the destructive aspect of life instead of the creative one. It was part of the educational process to make the children aware of the 'laws of development'.

Froebel now refers to the rhymes which were provided with the Gifts. There were two verses for each form (or shape) to be constructed. One verse in large letters, referred to the external characteristics of the object it represented and the second verse to 'inner meaning and connection'. The first verse was for the child and would be learned by heart, though Froebel is at pains to explain, that they need not be used provided the meaning of them was explained to the child, while the second verse was for the benefit of the adult, though more advanced children might profit from them. He emphasises that the learning off by heart of these verses should only be incidental. Insistence upon it would have the opposite effect from that which was desired. At any rate, the more the adult (and the child) played with the Gift, the more objects he would create, the more connections he would make, and the greater his own treasure of ideas would become and with it the search for new words. The player would eventually be able to expand these ideas to include human relationships, social life and moral issues. Thus Froebel puts before the reader the idea that this simple Gift is capable of representing all life and, provided it is used at the child's level of understanding, is an ideal educational instrument.

We remember that in the 1838 publication the emphasis regarding the 'Forms of Life' was on stories which linked the objects with real life situations (e.g. grandmother sat on a chair), stories which were made up as the adult played with the child. In this publication, however, the emphasis is on order of construction and ready-made verses. Froebel is aware of the danger of thoughtless imitation by the child, how much was he aware of thoughtless imitation by the adult? He clearly believed that he must provide a coherent blue-print for harassed and busy mothers. But did this not also encourage a slavish following of his instructions and therefore might it not also defeat his objectives? Is this the reason why he finally returned to the original publication of 1838 when he produced his final version?

The instructions for the use of the 'Forms of Beauty' follow a similar pattern. The adult is encouraged to experiment with the cubes first, then to consult the illustrations provided, compare the two and finally rebuild them according to instructions. Froebel, as indicated earlier, goes so far as to suggest with which finger tip of which hand one has to move which cube in order to move the top four cubes from the bottom four. Though irritatingly pedantic, it is based on Froebel's idea that nothing happens by chance or in an arbitrary fashion - everything has order and purpose. Each form develops from the previous one. No other solution is possible. Only the top four cubes are free to be moved, and, in Froebel's words, 'only the alternating actions of freedom and necessity produce a beautiful form'.[8]

Once the first form has been established, only the four outside cubes are moved and each cube to the same degree as the previous one. A pattern of ten forms is established, where forms Nos 1 and 5, and 6 and 10 are always identical. These forms more than any other, illustrate similarity and difference, law and order and are therefore an excellent way, in Froebel's opinion, to demonstrate that everything in life changes yet nothing is completely new.

There is one other aspect which was not brought out clearly in the 1838 version, but which receives detailed attention in the 1844 publication. Every Form of Beauty created is a part of a series. Just as Nos 1 and 5, and 6 and 10 are always the same, so are Nos 2 and 4, and 4 and 6 but in reverse. Froebel maintains that objects and events are not truly understood unless we also comprehend the reverse of them. Not until Piaget introduced 'the structural properties of thought' in his series of studies of childhood was 'reversibility' truly recognised as a major characteristic of cognition.[9]

The 'Forms of Knowledge' are treated much more scantily than in the original publication and references to the shape of a fraction as a means for recognition are only made in the accompanying verses. Froebel asserts that 'Number Forms' are self-explanatory.

The booklet closes with some general observations. Froebel mentions that if several children are playing with their Gifts, it is advisable to collect all the constructions and display them in order of difficulty so that the teacher can talk with the children about the ways and means by which another form could be created from the previous one. As is shown by the 1851 publication, this idea was abandoned in favour of creating 'a village' or 'a farm' using all the constructions made by each child where a more natural link between each individual construction could be made visible.

Froebel also mentions that constructions which were particularly liked by other children could be reproduced by them, accompanied by word and song. For it is 'word, object, activity, imagination, emotional involvement and thought which unites to a whole and renders the child's life complete.'[10] Here Froebel also sounds a word of warning. He says that it would have been very easy to elaborate on any of the forms given, but this might have been detrimental to the child's own powers of creation. Only when a child has created his own form should he be asked to imitate those of others and then imitation has to be an 'examining imitation' and not mere copying.

## The Final Version of 1851

The final version is essentially a reprint of the original one from 1838, but with additional instructions for Kindergarten teachers about the use of the Gift with a group of children as against the single child so far always mentioned.

As the original version has already been discussed, it will suffice to concentrate on the additions only.[11]

Froebel suggests, indeed insists, that not only must every child have his own Gift, but the teacher as well. This will avoid an unnecessary and arbitrary interference in the child's play-activities and help him to concentrate on, and pursue to the finish, the task in hand. This, Froebel believes, is important for the child's mental development in general as well as for his future life.

Children have to be shown how to open the box by sliding the lid vertically, as the retaining groove may easily be damaged if not operated carefully. If a mishap should occur, it is important to get the box mended as soon as possible, for a child must never be surrounded by broken objects, lest he become accustomed to broken things which, to a child, must be like a broken life. But until the box can be mended, and even after it has been mended, it should always be returned to the same child, not as a punishment, but so that he may learn to become and remain more careful.

Froebel emphasises once more that children must not just empty the content of the Gift box in any haphazard fashion onto their desks, but must start with the eight smaller cubes forming one big whole cube. Equally important, he says, is the development of each form from the previous one. Whilst in the 1844 version he gave the reason for this as the realization of 'wholeness' and 'the law of development', this time he argues that this will educate the child towards the appreciation that certain ideas, or thought processes, will lead to other, logically connected ideas and thus towards logical thinking.

All the work should be collected at the end of the lesson and exhibited on a central table. Children should now be encouraged to 'consider' each other's work and the teacher should combine the constructions in a 'travel-report' or any other connected story. Forms will then begin to appear in a different light to the children; they will talk about it and discover relationships previously not noticed. Froebel is in fact saying that imitation in play is not synonymous with copying, because it demands transformational activities. Froebel would maintain, and Piaget would agree, that one can only imitate what one knows.

As in the 1844 version, children should be encouraged to rebuild another child's creation, but - unlike the 1844 version - children should *not* be shown how these forms developed, so that the child who rebuilds them is forced to consider them in detail and to do his own thinking about them. Children should also be asked to work in groups, where one child builds a church, another the school etc. so that the whole objective has to be considered before the children start. A song about the village could be made up by the teacher and with the help of the children.

Only after all these exercises have been carried out, should children be asked to rebuild from the illustrations provided. This will help children to interpret drawings, make comparisons and pay attention to detail.

Froebel then concentrates on the 'Forms of Beauty' and explains to the Kindergarten teachers that these forms demand from the child an appreciation of order, symmetry and harmony. These forms cannot be interpreted in terms of usage and usefulness, yet they encourage an area of human development which is too often sadly neglected, that of careful consideration of detail and the restructuring of the whole from its parts. It brings in its wake an awareness of the 'inner' order of things. Each of these forms has an all-important centre from which everything radiates. It is not difficult to link this with one's own inner centre which finds expression in our behaviour.

A comparison of the three publications illustrates once again how Froebel is concerned with how much freedom and how much structuring has to be part of the play-activities with the Gifts. While in the first version the emphasis is placed on 'letting the child play with the bricks and build what he likes', asking the adult to make up stories according to the child's construction, the second version places the emphasis on showing mothers all the possibilities from the start and even provides a little verse to go with each construction. A hundred Forms of Beauty are carefully worked out and illustrated in the second version, none in the first. There is an atmosphere of urgency about the second version to get on with the teaching. Little room is given for 'free play', even other children's constructions should be used for imitation.

It is significant, that when Froebel published the third version, one year before he died, he based it on the original one of 1838. As if to emphasise his concern that more freedom be given within his structured play material, he adds that each teacher must have his own set of Gifts to play with, so as not to interfere with the children while they are playing.

Further study of the three publications of the third Gift reveals one other aspect of play with which Froebel is very much concerned. He is aware of the importance of imitation in play as an agent for learning, but not sure how it should be used.

How closely other children's work ought to be 'imitated' varied with the different publications, but judging from the final version, it seems that imitation, though still very important, was not to take place at the expense of understanding, reflection and re-creation. He therefore suggested that sometimes the forms to be imitated should be removed before the child started to rebuild them. It would force the child to build from memory, thus using mental images.

What Froebel does not seem to have realized, or at any rate does not make clear, is that even 'free representation of any objects from life' is an act of imitation. It presupposes a mental image, an image which is free from direct observation and which has therefore already been made into a generalised symbol. Piaget who devoted a whole book to the problem (*Play, Dreams and Imitation in Childhood*) states that

> With the mental image . . . imitation is no longer merely deferred but internalized, and the representation that it makes possible, thus dissociated from any external action in favour of the internal sketches of actions . . . is now ready to become thought.[12]

To Piaget the difference between play and imitation is crucial. In play, the primary objective is to mould reality to the demands of the player, whilst in imitation the mental structures of the player are subordinated to reality.

> . . . Play and imitation are significant primarily as cognitive activities in which assimilation and accommodation are decidedly not in balance. In play the primary object is . . . to assimilate reality to various schemas with little concern for precise accommodation to that reality . . . . Whilst in play there is primacy of assimilation over accommodation, in imitation on the other hand, it is accommodation which reigns supreme.[13]

When Sutton-Smith criticised Piaget on the grounds that since Piaget accounted for play's cognitive components as having been derived from copies of earlier accommodative behaviour (e.g. imitation) he had in fact developed a copy-theory of play, Piaget answered by stating this could not possibly be so, since he 'considered play a transformational activity'.[14] Piaget explains:

> . . . the reality that intelligence tries to grasp consists of a series of states (A,B,C, etc.) and transformations which modify these states (A into B, B into C, etc.)[15]

Piaget distinguishes two components. The figural component derived from perception, imitation and imagery, and the cognitive component which takes account of transformation and builds on actions (sensory-motor actions, interiorised actions, thought operations). The latter is not a matter of imitation but of mental construction. Figurative components are only useful when they are subordinated to the cognitive component, and 'play is an exercise of action schemes and therefore part of the cognitive component of conception'.[16]

Piaget thus puts the emphasis on 'action and construction' (overt and internalised) in play and not on the figural component. And so does Froebel:

> Imitative play in its most elementary and smallest beginnings demands a threefold exertion - namely: the effort to separate the action from the object, the special appreciation of this by free assimilation of the action, and the free representation of it from within by means of an unfamiliar action.[17]

## The Fourth Gift - a large wooden cube divided into eight large blocks (eight rectangular solids) where the length is twice its height and the width half of the large cube

The explanations of the fourth Gift appears in the *Sonntagsblatt* of 1838 and seems to be the only one Froebel ever published. It was reprinted in Lange's *Friedrich*

*Froebel Gesammelte Paedagogische Schriften*, and in Seidel's *Froebel's Paedagogische Schriften*, but generally received little attention from subsequent writers on Froebel.

There also exists an article for a newspaper, written in 1844 explaining the Gifts with some reference to the fourth and fifth Gifts. While it is not certain whether this article ever appeared in any of the papers at the time, it certainly was never published after Froebel's death. The reason for this may be found in the fact that the article was written in the third person. It appears as if another person is the writer, and not Froebel. Yet it is written in Froebel's handwriting. Of course, it is possible that Froebel copied the article from a newspaper. As sentence construction and vocabulary used are identical with those used in Froebel's writings in general, it is most likely that the article was composed by Froebel himself.

This article[18] gives us some clues as to Froebel's general thinking regarding the use of the Gifts which are not always to be found in the detailed explanations of and instructions in the Gifts. For example, he says that the third Gift should be used with children from three to five, though possibly also with a two year-old, but that if a child has worked through the exercises of one Gift and has started a new one, the previous Gifts should not be abandoned, but should be used by the child 'on a higher level' for 'education is a continuous process'.[19] Both the article as well as the explanations to the fourth Gift of 1838, have been used in this summary.

We remember that the third Gift consisted of a large cube which was divided into eight smaller cubes of equal size. The mathematical division of the third Gift was based on length, height and width, that is the large cube was subdivided by one cut in each direction - length, height, width - and it is these three aspects which have to be the basis for the next division of the cube. The large cube is now divided into eight equally long blocks where the length is twice its height and the width half of that of the large cube.

In his introduction to the fourth Gift, Froebel focuses our attention on one aspect of a child's make-up which hitherto he has not mentioned. He says that the child will by now have come to trust the adult (parents and teachers) and that it is of utmost importance not to give the child stones when he asks for bread, so we must be careful also to give him play-materials which are nourishing. This will only be achieved if the child realizes that what he has been offered will be for his own good.

Froebel then puts before us the notion that a child at this stage in his development looks constantly for something 'new'. Not something 'new' which has no connection with what is already known and would therefore only produce a barrier to learning, but 'the new in the old', which the child may look for in a different use of a familiar object, in unexpected characteristics of familiar events and also in new and different relationships with the people he knows, especially his parents and other adults. At this stage, and we have to remember that Froebel is talking of children aged about five, a child is not yet able to give account of these demands, but he expresses them in his constant demand for 'change'. It is therefore of great

Physical dexterity demands not just physical strength, but co-ordination of action. It is easier to grasp a ball than to let it go, easier to role it fast than to roll it slowly. To Froebel, unco-ordinated movements have to be made conscious before they can be co-ordinated. Therefore, even physical dexterity is ultimately a process which demands attention and reflection on action carried out.

Knowledge of objects and events too is gained by co-ordination and by making the details conscious. New knowledge has to be crystallised and differentiated before it can be incorporated into what is known already. Once the child knows that the ball always runs downhill, never uphill, Froebel can make a rhyme and compare it with the water of a stream.[21] This, of course, is open to rote-learning; the child can repeat the words without understanding what he says. Froebel therefore stresses the use of knowledge gained.

The use of knowledge gained involved abstraction, comparison and again, co-ordination. The knowledge that a ball always rolls downhill will also apply to an apple, but not to a key - though this may vary with angle of slope and weight of key. Cause and effect will have to be considered.

The way by which all this knowledge is gained, is important too, for it will eventually determine a person's attitude to life. If a child is educated in a classroom where events are predictable, where the next step in the learning process is determined by the previous step, where nothing is left to chance, law and order, beauty and harmony will affect the character of that person. It will lead to self-discipline and the structuring of the self free from pretence and falsehood, for arbitrary action by the learner will be out of keeping with his environment. Such structuring of the self presupposes freedom to act.

> Free choice, self-activity, the will, has been made conscious in the child while playing with the Gifts, because he was allowed to choose his occupations. But at the same time, no doubt, he has become aware of his dependence on others and the hindrance of obstacles . . . . Both will have produced on the one hand an awareness of himself as an individual, as an independent being, and on the other as a dependent, a part of a whole.[22]

Once more we encounter Froebel's notion that playing with the Gifts allows for 'freedom within certain laws'. Yet, the careful structuring of these play activities make us wonder whether we can still call it 'play'. Froebel himself seems to have had misgivings about this problem as early as 1840, for in that year, and after the publication of the fifth Gift, he introduces the Movement Games, where, so Froebel says, 'independence of actions plays a larger part'. The consideration of the Movement Games must therefore be our next concern.

1. Blochmann, 1965, p.49.
2. ibid.
3. Froebel, 1842, MS 8/47/29-94, p.78.
4. ibid, 1851, MS 19/12/1, p.1-11.
5. ibid, p.20.
6. ibid, p.30.

7. ibid, 1839, MS 19/8/8a, p.102.

8. ibid, 1844, p.21.

9. Flavell, 1963, p.7.

10. Froebel, 1844, p.39.

11. ibid, nd, MS 19/12/2, p.21-6.

12. Piaget, 1971, p.56.

13. Flavell, 1963, p.65.

14. Herron & Sutton-Smith, 1971, p.340.

15. Piaget *in* Herron & Sutton-Smith, 1971, p.337.

16. ibid, p.338.

17. Froebel, 1845, MS 19/8/5/122-127.

18. ibid, 1844, MS 19/8/2.

19. ibid, p.5.

20. Froebel *in* Lange, 1874, p.148.

21. Froebel, 1842, MS 8/47/29-94, p.65.

22. ibid, p.79.

# Chapter 6
# The Movement Games and Occupations

Froebel provides three reasons for the use of the Movement Games. First of all, he points out that some of the games played with the ball were already movement games of some kind (e.g. going for a walk), and therefore, the following series of games were only a logical extension of the former. Secondly, while play with the Gifts tied the child to an object Froebel believed that there must of necessity be games where activity is expressed by the player himself. 'In these games independence is more emphasised.'[1] Finally, it is not sufficient to provide material for the child which is in accord with his externally visible ability, but it is also the educator's task to 'detect the hidden (inner) development of the child and to fulfil these demands'.[2] These hidden developments could best be detected by providing an opportunity for expression from within.

Froebel is in fact saying that the use of the Gifts placed the emphasis on the structuring from without and that a play activity had to be introduced which allowed the child more freedom to express what was within him. As we shall see, these Movement Games were not without a certain structure, but it was a structure which not only allowed, but indeed encouraged, a more spontaneous behaviour. Froebel hoped that through these games 'the inner life of the child, and his inner development could really be expressed'.[3]

It was part of Froebel's philosophy that the meaning of life was to be found in the interpretation of the 'inner' and the 'outer'. The inner life of man, just like the outer world of nature, were both governed by the same laws, the laws of God. The life in nature and the action of man united the two. 'All life is unity'. It meant that nature (the life in nature) is the expression of God (an externalisation of his laws), and it demonstrated at the same time that the spiritual can only be made manifest in something external, in the 'outer'. Because there is only one law governing all life, what is true of God, his spirit and nature, must also be true of man, his inner life and his actions.

Just as God mediates through life in nature and man through his actions, so does the child in his play. But every act of mediation presupposes a medium by which the process can be carried out. Froebel realized that the medium to illustrate 'life, beauty

*Circle Games at the Michaelis Kindergarten, London, 1908.*

and knowledge', as well as the 'laws of life' had to be an objective one, one which would be experienced through the senses. The medium was provided by the Gifts.

Froebel's well-known but little understood saying - 'To make the inner outer and the outer inner' - is nowhere better explained than in his play theory. While the child expresses his inner life in his play, he simultaneously opens up the world to his own understanding. To hold a ball tightly at one moment, to let it go the next and then hold it again, not only gave expression to a child's inner life, namely 'what he has felt already many times at his mother's breast',[4] but also strengthened and clarified for him one of man's basic concepts of oneness and separation, of having, not having and finding; of present, past and future. The 'world' is now represented in the play-objects, and the value of play is to be found in the alternating changes between outer representation of the inner and the inner realization of the outer. But because the medium (the Gifts) may not allow full expression of the child's inner life and his potentials, Froebel encourages the use of the Movement Games, which, he believes, will lead to the development of more concise language and a greater social awareness.

Froebel starts off by considering the movements of the ball, 'for these are the roots for all Movement Games'. A ball can be made to walk, run, roll, fall, hop, jump, turn, swing, circle, fly, approach, recede, come, go, disappear, re-appear and unite things.

The first activities then were games where children were standing and walking, for a state of rest is the origin of movement. Even a child's first steps produce joy, for it not only makes the child aware that he is able to move, but able to move from one place to another and therefore able to achieve something.

A very young child, just beginning to walk, usually moves towards something, probably to hold on to it. Yet, whatever object he eventually reaches, be it a table, a chair or a bench, it will have a pointed corner, a sharp edge, a soft seat, etc., and it is wise for the adult to name these.

> This is not a matter of developing speech, but of perceiving objects, their parts and characteristics. It is the rich treasure of such experiences which develops speech of necessity . . . .[5]

Just as play presupposes an active and rich life, so does language. The truth of such statements is not understood even in our time, where 'Language Enrichment Programmes' concentrate on words to improve 'attention, speech, structure and vocabulary',[6] rather than on a richer and more meaningful life in terms of children's own actions which provide the basis for a more extensive and deeper structure of language.

Froebel realized that effective language development was not a matter of teaching words, but of providing experiences which demand speech. Because a word is already a generalisation, referring to a group of objects and not to a single object, it was imperative that the emphasis was on the many different experiences which made the word meaningful.

Tolstoy, in his educational writings, says that children often have difficulty in learning a new word not because of its sound but because of the concept to which the word refers. There is a word available nearly always when the concept has matured.[7]

Froebel's thinking on language development is much more in line with Vygotsky and Piaget than with Chomsky and is supported by Nixon's research results in children's classification skills, where she found:

> ... many instances of inconsistency between action and speech in young children, the general principle being that children could accurately group, match and order objects before they had sufficient grasp of language to explain what they had done, and why.[8]

To Froebel it was the experience, clarified by language, which constituted the growth of intelligence:

> Each new perception is a new discovery in the child's small but rich world; for example that one can walk around a chair, stand in front, behind and beside it, but that one can only walk parallel to a wall-bench.[9]

These simple beginnings introduce children to 'Wander Games' and because it is seemly and right to visit somebody on our walks, to 'Visiting Games'. Customs of greeting and invitation are adhered to and at the end of each game, children are asked to name, in the right order, the people they have met in their wanderings or to describe events, imaginary or real, experienced on their 'Visiting Games'.

Some of the Visiting Games are carried out by children along a figure of eight, this leads to the 'Representational Games' (The Snail, The Mill, The Wheel etc.) Not the most obvious characteristics are represented, but those which need more careful observation if they are to be noticed, e.g. the spiral in the snail, the fast-moving outer part of the wheel together with the slow-moving inner part. These Movements Games culminate in the 'Crown and Circle Games', which are the equivalence of the 'Forms of Beauty' in the Gifts. Several of these games, which were never published, can be found in Froebel 1842: MS 8/47:82-88.

Thus, Froebel succeeds in innovating a form of child-movement which is related to the child's life rather than to isolated exercises of certain limbs. It involves children in walking, running, hopping and jumping, turning on the spot, lifting one or both arms, lateral trunk movements, standing and walking on the tip of one's toes, and so on. Movements are based on how we saw wood, how we swim, how birds fly, tying a wreath, planting seeds, working in the garden, feeding chickens, cat and mouse. Exercises, with very rare exceptions, were related to a simple verse explaining or describing a real life situation. It was essential that the whole person was involved in these exercises, the senses and the mind as well as the limbs. Froebel considered physical exercises (Turnen) as unsuitable for children in the Kindergarten because they were too one-sided, 'while in play and games the imagination was involved together with body and mind'.[10]

At the same time, the initially individual behaviour of the child in the Wander and Visiting Games - where children were free to walk where they liked, visit who they wished and could take whatever route they wanted - extended progressively into games of a social character, where other children's wishes, demands and behaviour had to be taken into consideration.

> These games cultivate, as the expression of a healthy inner life, a beautiful bearing of the whole body as well as its individual parts. They educate towards language and song, awaken attention, a sense of law and order, decency and beauty. Above all they effect a happy and satisfying 'living together', the origins of infinite, human and Christian virtues.[11]

Very little attention has been paid to these Movement Games, yet as Froebel himself maintained, they are a necessary extension of the Gifts. The popularity of these games is recorded in a report of one of the earliest Kindergartens[12] where children began each day with a prayer and a song followed by the Movement Games.[13] By putting the emphasis on movement and a freer and more imaginative kind of representation of life around the child, they encourage these areas which Froebel critics maintain are neglected in the use of Gifts.

> ... these occupations have theoretical as well as practical value, value for the inner and innermost personal as well as for the external, social life. They have aesthetic as well as scientific meaning because they carry the essentials and the germ of them, within them. They are important as regards the person himself (morally) as well as his intellect. They are equally important for mind and heart, as well as for life, the deed.[14]

It seems appropriate to mention Froebel's Occupations in conjunction with the Movement Games, for they, like the latter, served the function of giving scope for expression and allowed for freedom to experiment. Children were provided with scissors and paper, sticks and threads of wool, clay and wax, peas and shells, sand and stones. They were encouraged to build, construct and model, to weave and sew, to cut out and to paste. Except for a short article on 'Paper Folding', published in 1850, and on 'Stick-Laying', published after his death, Froebel left us no record in detail of how these activities were supposed to be carried out. This seems to be significant, considering that Froebel took such meticulous care over the explanations of the Gifts. A letter, dated 7 October 1844, bears witness to the fact that many activities and games were 'being used in Froebel's Institutions which he has not yet published'.[15] Froebel lived for another seven years. Why did he leave us no detail?

Froebel's followers worked diligently on the details of these Occupations after his death. The results of this diligence were carefully executed paper-cutting, paper-weaving and pin-pricking exercises, performed by children of suitable age. The final rejection of Froebel's play activities was primarily the result of people's awareness that the insistence on such fine and careful work by young children was not in their interest. Did Froebel suspect that exactly this might happen if he worked out such detailed instructions?

He obviously believed that the general framework of his Gifts and Occupations, which he mentioned in several publications, would suffice. It was based on his philosophy of 'unity', was mathematical in structure and followed a logical progression. It starts with three-dimensional objects, (the ball and the cube), which are developed into representation and use of area (flat wooden tablets of different mathematical shapes), then lines (sticks) and finally the point (peas, stones).

Three-dimensional bodies are first whole, then divided. Area, though at first still three-dimensional, is already indicated in the division of the whole. Lines are physically represented by sticks but is an abstraction of the lines as indicated by the edges of the cube.

Froebel believed that the processes of knowing were based on taking in, assimilation, and giving out, expression. Froebel maintained that the effectiveness of each of these activities depended on the intimate connection with the other. To Froebel, knowledge is information taken in and assimilated in relation to what is already known. But information only becomes knowledge if we can see its relation to other things and facts. In order to bring out the individual characteristics of a thing most clearly, Froebel introduced his 'doctrine of opposites' to aid analysis and recognition. We analyse so that we may comprehend and comprehend only in as much as we are able to reconstruct in thought that which we have analysed. This mental reconstruction is therefore the final aim in Froebel's theory of play and because children at this stage understand more easily when using concrete material, Froebel invented the 'Occupations'.

Starting with the point this time, the whole process is reversed. Paper pricking (the point) leads to the drawing of lines, using squared paper, resulting in planning grids, for which Froebel has been severely criticised.[16] But these grids were extensively used by Frank Lloyd Wright in his architecture. He had experienced Froebel's Kindergarten education in his childhood and planning grids are now used as an integral part of study by students of architecture. These grids not only accommodate and resolve systems of function and technology within a building, but also provide a holistic dimension in the Froebelian sense. The holistic dimension of Froebel's Gifts and Occupations find expression in Frank Lloyd Wright's prairie period of architecture in particular, where the interior and exterior of his buildings show a common identity when external symmetry determines internal organisation.[17]

In Froebel's Occupations, the drawing of lines and planning grids are extended into paper folding and cutting out shapes. This is continued with activities using a flexible thread, then 'Stick-weaving and Interlacing', followed by three-dimensional work in wax, loam, clay (soft materials) and finally potatoes, turnip stalks and soft wood.

All these Occupations have mainly to do with expression, while the Gifts are predominantly means for taking in and assimilation. The former provide for invention and skill, the latter for discovery, insight and ideas. But because assimilation and expression have to go hand in hand, the Occupations have to be used at the same time and in conjunction with the Gifts. Some connections are evident at once: work with clay, wax and wood go with the first six Gifts as far as exercises in solid form are concerned; Paper folding and paper cutting go with the tablets for work on surfaces; exercises with the flexible thread and stick weaving with sticks and rings. In choosing the Occupation we must look at the nature of the exercise demanded by the Gift exercise. If, for example, the Gift exercise is concerned with number work, mat-plaiting or stick weaving, where numbers are used in groups, would be the appropriate sequence. If the Gift exercise is concerned with the Forms of Beauty, colour work or paper-mosaic work would be a suitable Occupation to choose.

If we asked again, whether all these activities could be considered play we notice that different activities within Froebel's total system of play emphasise different criteria. The Movement Games, for example, provide more freedom for the child than the activities with the Gifts. At the same time, they include the element of tension between the familiar and the new, the known and the unknown. The mere description of these activities does not enable us to draw conclusions as regards the intentions and motives of the player to decide whether children were sufficiently motivated to prolong their play so as to 'find fulfilment in the ongoing activity'. There are, however, accounts which illustrate how much children enjoyed playing with the Gifts and how children followed Froebel home after a day's work in the Kindergarten, so that they might continue playing with the Gifts in his own house. This was probably not true of all the children nor at all times, but it seems to indicate that this last criterion was at least fulfilled some of the time. It now remains to be seen whether a more complete integration of all these criteria can be seen in Froebel's last and educationally probably most important series of play activities as outlined in the Mother Songs.

1. Froebel, 1842, MS 8/47/29-94, p.80.
2. Froebel *in* Lange, 1874, p.183.
3. Froebel, 1842, MS 8/47/29-94, p.80.
4. Froebel *in* Lange, 1874, p.28.
5. ibid, p.187.
6. Gahagen, 1970.
7. Vygotsky *in* De Cecco, 1969, p.59.
8. Nixon, 1971, p.77.
9. Froebel *in* Lange, 1874, p.187.
10. Froebel, L., nd, MS 3/15b/274.
11. Froebel, 1842, MS 8/47/29-64, p.90.
12. At Gotha, 1847.
13. Erdmann & Michaelis, 1839, MS 21/20.
14. Froebel, 1841, MS 1/7/24-53, p.33.
15. ibid, 1844, MS 19/8/2.
16. Hanschmann, 1875, p.328.
17. MacCormac, 1974, pp.29-50.

# Chapter 7
# The Mother Songs - 1844

The complete title of *The Mother Song Book* reads:

> Come let us live for our children. Mother Songs, as well as Songs for Games with body limbs and senses. For the early and uniting care of childhood. A Family Book by Friedrich Froebel.

It seems almost inevitable that the educator who began his professional career with the universal exposition of *The Education of Man*, then developed his ideas about the education of pre-school-age children, should conclude his most creative chapter in life by paying attention to the particular of children's first learning, to the stage of development where the child is not yet able to manipulate objects meaningfully and successfully himself.

Froebel recognised that before the stage of active manipulation of objects, there is a time when the child experiences the world primarily through his senses and through the manipulation of his own limbs. And because the processes of education begin on the day the child is born, it is imperative that some guidance be given to mothers about these very first interactions between mother and child. This Froebel did in his 'Mother Songs', published in 1844. Its complete title, so cumbersome and offputting to many, sets the scene and provides the aim. They are songs to cosset the child, but at the same time to provide games for the use of the senses, the limbs and the body. It is a 'family book' for the purpose of 'the early, continuous and uniting care of childhood'; a family book which might be read and used by mothers or fathers, grandparents or older siblings, all of whom would be united by the common activity and the common goal, the welfare and education of the youngest in the family.

The book itself was a 'family affair' of the Keilhau circle. Froebel wrote the words, the drawings were provided by Friedrich Unger (1811-1858), the Keilhau artmaster, an old pupil of the school who had returned to Keilhau after his studies at the Kunstakademie in Munich and who later became curator of the Germanische Museum at Nurmberg, and the music composed by Robert Kohl (1813-1880), parson and teacher at Keilhau.

Ida Seele, a student of Froebel's at the time,[1] recorded how she had to sing several versions of each song before it was finalised and put on paper, and how Froebel, Middendorff and Kohl had tried to find a melody for each verse which would be a 'picture in sound' for the underlying text. Yet the task given to Kohl was easy compared with that given to Unger. Froebel was difficult to please, and only the best, the most perfect was good enough to be presented to children. Just as Froebel employed the most artistic joiner in the area to produce the Gifts, mathematically accurate, beautifully finished and perfectly packed, so Froebel also installed his own lithographical press for the printing of the book. All the drawings were illustrations of real life: the children of the Keilhau community were the subjects, and the hands of the students the medium through which the finger games and the objects of Unger's drawings were tried out.

> What patience, what diligence, what cost, what sacrifice of strength and sleep was paid for the Mother Songs. How Froebel and Middendorff worked on them, how much care and finally at what great expense were the drawings produced.[2]

If the meaning of life could only be found in the law and order of nature, which was also the law of God, accuracy, order, beauty and meaning were fundamental to anything presented to the children.

The book contains fifty play-songs which aim at providing exercises for body and limbs to be carried out by mother and child and at the same time it provides a symbolic introduction to the abstract values in life. Each play-song is printed on one page surrounded by pictures illustrating the song in many different ways. Incorporated into each series of pictures is usually a drawing of a pair of hands, illustrating the kind of hand or finger exercise which can be carried out with the song. There are two verses on each page, one in large print to be sung to the child and one in smaller print serving as a short explanation about the deeper meaning of each song, for the mother. A more detailed explanation for each song is given at the end of the book.

## Aims and Purpose

Those who accord the book only a casual glance, will find the pictures fuzzy, the songs trite and the explanations too elaborate and not easy to understand. Only careful attention to and reflection on the details will enable the student to comprehend and appreciate the pedagogical riches in the book. Froebel himself had no doubt as to the book's significance.

> I have recorded the most important aspects of my educational theory in this book; it is the starting point for an education based on nature, for it shows the way. How the germinal buds of human potentials have to be nourished and supported if they are to develop healthily and completely.[3]

In the explanation to the Mother Songs, at the end of the book, we are able to unravel three threads which Froebel takes as his guide lines. He aims at the introduction of physical play between mother and child involving limbs and the senses, knowledge about the world around the child and the symbolic meaning of life. He says that the strengthening of the limbs, body and senses will lead to a more purposeful use of them, and this in turn to an awareness of things as they are and the consideration of them. Consideration and awareness of separate objects prepares for the search for their connections and for the whole. Thus, physical activity is the basis for mental activity, for 'outer arrangements of things into groups and classes will lead to inner comparisons and judgements', which develop our powers of comprehension and understanding. Once we have developed these powers of comprehension, we are no longer satisfied with perceptual judgements but ask for the reasons and origins underlying things and events, which in turn develop our powers of logical thinking, culminating in abstract thinking.[4]

It would be easy to find a comparable statement in Piaget's writings for each of Froebel's statements made in this last paragraph. The comparison of the stages of mental development given by Froebel with those by Piaget: sensory-motor, pre-operational (pre-conceptual, intuitive, symbolic), concrete operational and formal operational, shows such similarities that they may be described as identical.

Piaget begins his description of the growth of intelligence, like Froebel, by emphasising the tools which the new-born baby has available for his learning: the limbs, body and senses. Piaget says that we can only find a very limited number of behavioural systems on the day a child is born. These are sucking, grasping, looking, listening, vocalising and bodily movements. At first,

> . . . the child looks for the sake of looking, grasps in order to grasp, etc. Then there is an accidental co-ordination between one schema and another (the child looks by chance at the hand which grasps, etc.) and finally, fixation . . .[5]

Though co-ordination between two schemas may be accidental in the first place, it soon leads to discrimination and intention. The human infant ceases to be a responder and becomes an initiator of activities which one or several of his schemas anticipate.[6]

The most important achievement of the young child at the sensory-motor stage is the establishment of the idea of the permanence of an object, even when the object is visually no longer in front of him. Piaget concludes: '. . . activity of this stage . . . is identical from the functional point of view with that of intelligence.'[7]

Froebel's emphasis on activity as a means for learning is supported by the argument that it will lead to 'an awareness of things as they are'. Piaget called it the pre-operational stage (including the intuitive and symbolic stage), because children at this stage judge things, objects and events on a perceptual level, on a level 'as things are'. One of the most pronounced characteristics of pre-operational thinking is the child's tendency to 'centre' his attention on one striking feature of the object (or action) to the exclusion of any other important aspects and by so doing distort his reasoning. The child at this stage is unable to 'de-centre' and to take other criteria into consideration which might compensate for the distorting effects of the single centration. 'Things are what they appear to be in immediate, egocentric perception: and insubstantial phenomena are substantiated as quasi-tangible entities.'[8]

Froebel says that the consideration of separate objects 'prepares for the search for their connection'. Piaget says that the ability to perceive objects and events in relationship to each other is not fully established until children have achieved 'reversibility', usually at the stage of concrete operations.

The stage of concrete operations is marked by the child's ability to perform mental operations (logical and mathematical) on his immediate environment. Freed from the bonds of perception, he is now able to construct and re-construct systems of class simultaneously, without forgetting one attribute while considering another. 'Operations are a continuation of actions' says Piaget,[9] because they originate from quite elementary activities like putting things in piles, separating piles into lots, making comparisons and so on. But it is the slowly developing ability to *reverse* thought processes which characterises 'operations' as a whole and which allows children at this stage to comprehend and understand, leading them to ask for the reasons underlying things and events. Froebel said about this stage that the child's activity in arranging objects into groups and classes will lead to comparisons and this in turn will lead to the development of the child's powers of comprehension and understanding. Once a child has reached this stage, he will no longer be satisfied to understand things as they are, he will search for 'what they might have been'. This is the stage of abstract thinking, Piaget calls it the stage of formal operations, where children begin to be able to make use of hypothetical reasoning, where their thinking is concerned with propositions rather than with physical situations and where they are eager to deal with the conceivably possible rather than just the actual.

Though Froebel did not name each stage, the order of them together with their characteristics are the same as those given by Piaget.

Further careful study of Froebel's explanations in his *Mother Song Book* however reveals that the education of man, at every level, involves more than a mere rational appreciation of life. He continues his explanations by saying that as our mind turns objects into images, so images are turned into symbols, and it is the symbolic which allows us to grasp the essence of matter as part of a spiritual whole. Froebel's explanations relating to the comparison between the dovecot and the child's spirit and his home, as outlined in this chapter, provides an illuminating example of the use of symbolism as a teaching aid. But before introducing these examples, it will profit us to examine Froebel's ideas on the use of the symbolic and the surmise in more detail.

Froebel uses the symbolic in education to provide the means by which to illuminate the deeper meaning of life. God, the Creator, the Almighty, the Spirit, in the sense of the Romantics, can only be comprehended in terms of his creation (nature) and in terms of man's own actions and experiences. As man's highest activity is to be found in his search for knowledge and for truth, that is education, education cannot function without the symbol. Education using such 'natural' symbols, which in Froebel's opinion can be understood at least at the level of the surmise, helps to interpret such direct experiences (e.g. nature and man's actions) and in so doing creates the ideal and pure *Gestalt*.[10]

Though Froebel's explanation to the Mother Songs ultimately have a deeply religious significance, the use of the symbolic is not only a means for providing a concrete example for spiritual matters, for making 'unity (and ultimately God) explicit in diversity' in its varied manifestations, but is also used to fulfil a psychological function. Froebel believed that the inner life of man is given expression in his actions and therefore that these actions in themselves were symbolic and contributed to a person's development of his mental structures provided they were recognised as being symbolic of a person's inner life by that same person. Finally, the symbolic was also used to illustrate philosophical concepts like perseverance, truthfulness, fairness and so on, in a way which can produce the beginning of an understanding even in young children. Of course, there is much more to the concept of truthfulness, for example, than is being expressed in the song 'The Fish in the Brook'. The symbolism used (the clear water of the stream) provides us with the surmise of what truthfulness is all about, rather than with factual elaborations, but then Froebel maintained that knowledge was made up of cognizance *and* the surmise.

Our current emphasis in the philosophy of education on the 'rational man' forgets, or conveniently ignores, that man is *more* than rational. Commitment, compassion, responsibility can well be explained in rational terms, but as King points out, it is not the only way to cultivate it.

> Nor indeed can we assess responsibility only in rational terms. If Christianity made a point different from the contribution of Greek philosophy, this is it.[11]

Froebel's system of education was carefully structured and rational in most aspects, and in those areas where he is charged with 'metaphysical speculations', as in his teaching about the meaning of life to young children, Froebel argues that whatever man is capable of doing and thinking in later life must at least be a surmise when a child is young. Nothing can grow unless there is at least a germ, a seed from which it can originate, and equally nothing can germinate unless the seed is given its correct nourishment and encouraged to grow. It is for this reason that Froebel in all his educational endeavours puts so much emphasis on the teaching of the meaning of life, even when the child cannot possibly grasp it intellectually. The fostering of the presentiment, of the surmise was paramount in his teaching and symbolism was the essential medium through which to achieve it.

> The wakening, strengthening, care, development, training . . . of the child's presentiment, is therefore the most important, the most difficult but also the most rewarding educational task.[12]

Froebel believed that there could be no understanding, no new learning, no change from a precept to a concept unless the surmise of it existed.

This argument, however convincing, presents the teacher with the problem of teaching, or at least providing the conditions for development in an area where very little, if anything at all, can be understood by the learner. Piaget's work on concept development indicates the futility of introducing areas of knowledge to children at a time when basic concepts are lacking. Yet we also have to recall and reflect on Luria's three-stage process in the development of the regulatory function of language. He places the first and initial stage at a time when language has no relevance to the child, the second stage at a time when it accentuates the vigour of an ongoing activity and only the last stage at a time in which the semantic value of the language units used become relevant. Very few people nowadays would not encourage, foster and support the child's efforts in the first two stages when the child is not able to attach meaning to language used.[13]

The 'metaphysical speculation' of which Froebel is frequently accused should therefore be directed against his basic assumption of the existence of a deity rather than the means by which this assumption is conveyed to children. For if his assumption is correct, his method of teaching it is as sound, or as misplaced, as our current teaching of language to young children.

It is therefore not surprising that Froebel's educational aims in the Mother Songs are not only directed towards physical play and knowledge of the environment, but extend to include the attempt to foster the surmise of the deeper meaning of life. It is illustrated in any one of the fifty songs and best demonstrated if we taken one or two of them and look at them in detail.

## *The Charcoalburner*, a symbol of the importance of the seemingly insignificant

The hands are placed together, fingertips to fingertips, palm to palm and thumb to thumb, fingers straight. The wrists are now moved away from each other so that the palms separate while the fingertips remain together so that a triangular shape is created. The two thumb-tips also remain together and with the base of the thumbs now apart, form a smaller triangle within the large triangle. Up to this point, it is a simple agility movement involving hands and wrists. The end product is in the shape of the charcoalburner's hut as in the picture.

This simple play with hands and fingers, Froebel now connects, in his endeavour for unity, with the teaching of knowledge about the world around the child. The verse to be used with the child tells him about the size of the hut, the craftsman and his sons who live in it and what they are doing. They may only be making coal, but without it, the blacksmith would not be able to bend his iron and he (the child) would then lack knife, fork and spoon. Thus, says Froebel to the child, let us welcome the charcoalburner and his work, for he enables us to enjoy our food. Then already moving to the symbolic he adds that, though his face may be black, it does not harm his heart. (Froebel frequently emphasised that we have to beware of judging from outer appearances and that what matters most is a person's 'inner life'.)

The three drawings illustrate the three scenes mentioned in the verse. They are scenes from life with which the child may be familiar. The charcoalburner working with his two sons in front of their hut, the blacksmith and his apprentice in the smithy, and finally the mother with the child on her lap feeding the child with a spoon. The charcoalburner's hut is placed in the middle of the forest and the straightness of the

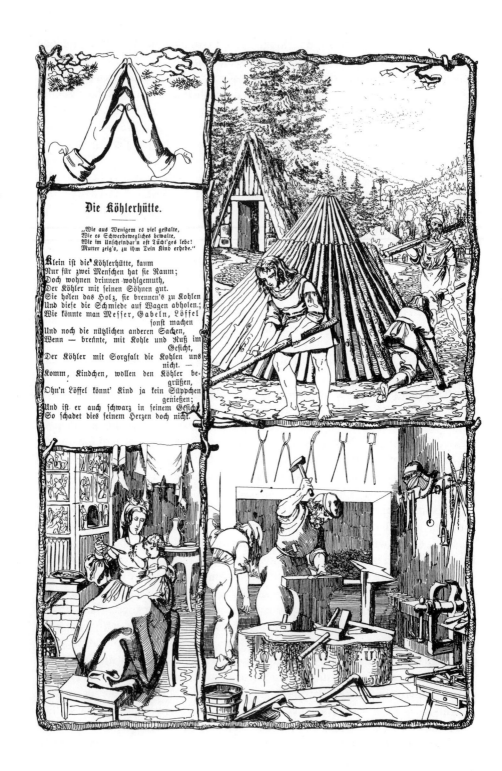

## Die Köhlerhütte.

„Wie aus Wenigem es viel gestalte,
Wie es Schwerbewegliches bewalte,
Wie im Unscheinbar'n oft Tücht'ges lebe!
Mutter zeig's, zu ihm Dein Kind erhebe."

Klein ist die Köhlerhütte, kaum
Nur für zwei Menschen hat sie Raum;
Doch wohnen drinnen wohlgemuth,
Der Köhler mit seinen Söhnen gut.
Sie holen das Holz, sie brennen's zu Kohlen
Und diese die Schmiede auf Wagen abholen;
Wie könnte man Messer, Gabeln, Löffel
                              sonst machen
Und noch die nützlichen anderen Sachen,
Wenn — brennte, mit Kohle und Ruß im
                              Gesicht,
Der Köhler mit Sorgfalt die Kohlen uns
                              nicht. —
Komm, Kindchen, wollen den Köhler be-
                              grüßen,
Ohn'n Löffel könnt' Kind ja kein Süppchen
                              genießen;
Und ist er auch schwarz in seinem Gesicht,
So schadet dies seinem Herzen doch nicht.

quick-growing conifers is repeated in the straightness of the timber used for the construction of the hut as well as in the stakes which form the triangular woodpile, ready for burning. The hut too is triangular with a rectangular door. Both these basic shapes are repeated in the picture of the smithy, the triangular shapes by a row of fire tongs hanging above the fire, and the rectangle by the fire opening. But the rectangular shape of the charcoalburner's hut is now repeated in a horizontal position, for the fire opening in the smithy is twice as long as it is high. Here we notice one of Froebel's principles, to demonstrate new knowledge in many different ways. These two basic shapes (the triangle and the oblong) are then combined in the third picture where the two openings in the living-room stove - one for drying wood and the other for keeping the coffee warm and making roast-apples - are square at the base and semi-circular at the top. The roundness of the semi-circle is already indicated in the waterbut in the smithy and in the huge block of wood on which the anvil rests. Iron instruments are to be found in all three pictures. What is apparently new in a picture can be found as an indication in the previous picture. All the people illustrated are working for the good of the other. The charcoalburner for the blacksmith, the blacksmith for the mother and child, and the mother for the child.

There is also a certain order prevailing in each picture. The wooden stakes in the woodpile are evenly spaced, the tools in the smithy hung up side by side for easy availability, and the washing drying beside the stove in the third picture, neatly arranged and spread out. The details, encouraging conversation and explanation by the mother from which the child might learn, are simple, accurate and beautifully executed. Each drawing is complete in itself and yet linked by ideas to form a unified whole.

The unified whole is the idea that important things have small beginnings, that first impressions may deceive, that outer appearances may hide true values. Froebel explains this for the benefit of mothers at the end of the book. Here he uses the hands as well as the charcoalburner as symbols to illustrate the 'true and inner meaning' of the song and play. Froebel urges mothers to reflect for a moment on the simple hand movement just carried out, what beautifully constructed and versatile instruments our hands are. No wonder he says, that an Englishman has written a whole book about the wonders of the hand and how it best demonstrated God's love and care for us. Though there are only two hands with two sets of four fingers, which correspond to each other in mirror fashion, so many things can be done with them, so many things can be represented with them by the child. The hut of the charboalburner, for example, the door, but also the wood-pyramid which the charcoalburner has to build in order to regulate the burning successfully. The hand is capable of so many good deeds and Froebel urges mothers to make children aware of this from an early age onwards so that they 'may not harm their hands nor themselves through them'. 'And as you teach your child to respect his own hands, teach him also to respect those who work with their hands.'[14]

Froebel reminds mothers that those who provide shelter, food and clothing for us deserve our gratitude. This gratitude has to be woken early in young children and

## Das Taubenhaus.

„Was das Kind im Innern füh[l]
    Gern es auch im Äußern spiel[t]
Wie's Täubchen fliegt in's Weite,
Macht's Ausgehn Kindern Freude,
Wie's Täubchen kehrt in's Haus zurück,
Wendt's Kindchen heimwärts bald den B[lick]
Zu Haus laß Pfleg' es finden,
Gefundenes zu winden
In einen bunten Kranz,
Was sich getrennt ließ finden,
Erzählung mags verbinden:
So wird das Leben ganz."

Ich öffne jetzt mein Taubenhaus,
Die Täubchen fliegen froh hinaus;
Sie fliegen hin auf's grüne Feld,
Wo's ihnen gar zu wohl gefällt.
Doch kehr'n sie heim zu guter Ruh,
So schließ' ich wieder mein Häuschen

must include gratitude towards the most humble of labourers who work for the good of the community. However shoddy and black the charcoalburner's dress may be, mothers ought to remember and recall the story of the nobleman and the two princes and how a charcoalburner saved the two princes from the evil hands of the nobleman because 'the charcoalburner's heart beat true for innocence, virtue and right'. Thus, the hands and the charcoalburner become the mediators between the 'outer and inner life of man', and the symbols which make objective what is subjective, visible that which is invisible.

Here is another example.

*The Dovecot*, a symbol of men's search for the absolute in the transitory, for the universal in the particular, for unity in the parts

The play activity involves the child's arms, hands and fingers. The left arm is held vertically to represent the pole on which the dovecot is built, and the hands form the shape of a cube representing the dovecot. The fingers of the left hand forming the top of the dovecot are raised to let the pigeons out and closed when they have returned home. When the pigeons have left the cot, the fingers of both hands can be used to represent the movements of the flying pigeons. So that both arms may be developed equally, the actions of each should be changed over from time to time.

The picture shows a dovecot in the foreground on the right with a farm house and a church in the background. Underneath the cot sits a mother with her child standing near and practising the finger games. Another mother with her child in her arms is placed in the centre-foreground. The baby is watching attentively some pigeons feeding on the path. An older child, turned away from its mother, is observing a titmouse sitting on the stump of a rotten branch of a tree. The stump is hollow and the titmouse obviously has its nest in there. On top of that tree is a bird-box, two older children are approaching from the background, absorbed in discussing their latest discoveries. In the far distance a farmer is ploughing his field.

The quadrangular shape of the dovecot is repeated in the shape of the large farmhouse and in the shape of the windows. The vertical line of the pole is repeated in the uprights of the fence, in the steeple and in the tree in the foreground; the horizontal line of the base of the cot, in the horizontal lines of the stone-wall and the fence. But geometrical shapes are overshadowed by movement. The two older children are coming towards us, some pigeons are approaching the cot and others are leaving, while a flock of birds is moving across the picture. But, as Froebel has expressed so often in the Movement Games,[15] the starting point of movement is rest. The sitting mother, the standing mother with her child on her arm, the perching titmouse, provide focal points of rest. Here we notice the use of one of Froebel's educational principles: the teaching by the 'law of opposites'.

In his explanations of the song and the picture, Froebel provides the mother with some ideas of what each person in the picture might be thinking, saying and doing. The boy, for example, observing the titmouse so intently that he is almost dropping

*The Mother Songs have here
become cosy nursery rhymes and
the emphasis is on simply keeping
the child happy.*

the apple from his hand, is wondering why the bird is turning away its head as if to disown the nest. The mother executing the finger games with her child is of course also talking to him. 'Where have you been and what did you see?' she asks him. 'Pigeons and chicken, geese and ducks, swallows and sparrows, larks and finches, ravens and magpies, water wagtails and titmice; bees, beetles, butterflies and bumble-bees', answers the child. Now the conversation turns towards the classification of these animals; where do we find each of them and how do they move? Some hop and others walk, some fly and others cannot, some swim and others do not. Are pigeons and hens birds? Yes,says the mother and gives as her criteria feathers, wings and two legs. 'But pigeons live in the dovecot and chickens don't fly', queries the child. This leads to the discussion of the problem of whether bees, beetles and butterflies are birds too, and this in turn to the introduction of the class of insects.

Froebel only indicates some of the possibilities of each picture, but this is sufficient to stimulate the reader to search for more. It was always his intention to educate mothers at the same time as children, and to exhaust the material provided would have limited the creative potential of mothers and children alike. Froebel, for example, makes no mention of the geometrical shapes, the movements, the obvious relationships between dovecot and pigeons, and farmhouse and children, the people's clothing and the feathers of the birds, the searching for food by the pigeons and the ploughing farmer, the nest of the titmouse and the cot of a baby, the stonewall and the wooden fence, the orchard and the forest, the twisted roots of trees and their knotted branches. Even then the possibilities of teaching children about the world they know are not exhausted. Yet, again, the exercises of the limbs linked with the teaching of the objective world leads to the fostering of the surmise.

Froebel maintained in his explanations that the child enjoys this game particularly because in the movements of the representation of the flying pigeons, he extends his own experience of coming and going and at the same time he reaches out for the life in nature. This is witnessed in his continuous demands to be let out of the house. Mothers are encouraged to meet this demand, for

> The child's spirit strives, even if not consciously, to find the permanent in the transient, the inner in the outer, the general in the specific, the whole in its parts, and finally, even if unconsciously, because he is a child of mankind, a divine spark, he must seek Unity, that which is complete in itself - God. Therefore foster this presentiment wherever you can, kindle the spark so that the feeling of it becomes an active realization.[16]

Thus, the flight of the pigeons is also a representation of the child's endeavour to know about life outside (nature) and that in turn, the symbol of his search for the permanent in life, for unity and ultimately for God.

Some people, says Froebel, will maintain that children at this stage are far too young for such matters; they will say: 'it is too early'. Too early? asks Froebel, how do we know? Where do we place the beginning of mental and spiritual developments? How do they make themselves manifest? God's world, he argues, gives evidence of a steady, unbroken development in anything we care to observe. The question we ought to ask is not *when* but *how*. The child learns walking before running, he tries to stand before he tries to walk, and he endeavours to strengthen his limbs and body before he endeavours to stand. If a child is encouraged to stand and walk before his limbs are strong, he will damage his bone structure; if encouraged too late, he will become clumsy in mind and body. The laws of mental development are no different from those of physical development. Therefore mothers ought to remember the interdependence of all the separate stages of development and to foster them all.

Froebel's education of the child in arms is concerned with the child's total development. It starts with what the child can 'do', uses this 'know-how to develop and strengthen the physical aspect of the child's existence, and links it at the same time with the knowledge of the child's immediate environment. This knowledge is made explicit in actions, pictures and words. But as each outer and concrete phenomenon has a deeper inner meaning, of which the teacher ought to be constantly aware, it must be part of the educational process. Because Froebel believes that the potential for understanding the inner meaning of our existence is present even in the very young child, he advocates the fostering of the surmise in its very beginning and in the only possible way, the symbolic. Thus, the charcoalburner becomes the symbol of the importance of the seemingly insignificance, and the flight of the pigeons, the flight of the human spirit in search for unity, harmony and peace. The detailed study of the other forty-eight songs in the Mother Songs reveals the same pattern.

How easily these songs and games are open to misuse is well illustrated by a booklet published in 1905 entitled *Songs and Games by Froebel*. The booklet consists of a selection of twenty of the Mother Songs with the pictures redrawn.

> ... in all previous translations the original German illustrations, which were issued in 1843, have been adhered to. These were appropriate for the student, but quite unsuited to English children of the present day. So the artists have been instructed in this edition to simplify and modernize their illustrations.[17]

The picture sequence for the charcoalburner (illustrating how one person relies upon the work and achievements of others) has been simplified to one picture illustrating the charcoalburner at work. The charcoalburner's hut and the woodpile are almost identical to the original. But the two sons helping their father (as mentioned in the song) are now two children where only one of them is working, while the younger one, possibly a girl, looks on. The woodpile is next to a tree with its branches overhanging the pile, bound to catch fire, once the pile is lit.

The picture of the dovecot is reduced to a dovecot in front of an inn with mother and two children in the foreground. One of the children looks up at their mother and the other at the inn. There is no movement of coming and going, no hint of exploration, no titmouse attentively observed by a child, no suggestion of any other animals (either in word or in drawing) which provided the intellectual extension in the original.

The translation of the songs shows the same kind of superficiality.
'And though he is sooty, never mind,
The charcoalburner is good and kind.'[18]
Froebel's teaching point, that outer appearances may deceive, is not only lost, but the impression is given that the charcoalburner should not really be black and dirty, but it 'does not matter'. To Froebel every word, every gesture, every detail mattered. 'Never mind' was not part of his vocabulary because it was alien to his thinking.

The Mother Songs have now become cosy nursery rhymes where the emphasis is on keeping the child happy.

> Keep this book by you, and when the next wet day comes, the baby is crying because he has nothing to do, show him how to amuse himself; and if you don't know how, just open this book and see.[19]

Froebel's educational aims for young children, to achieve harmony through knowledge has now been replaced by 'achieving happiness through amusement'. No longer are we concerned with the careful observation of animals, with the teaching of respect for others, including those who perform menial tasks for our well-being, with the intellectually demanding task of classification and seriation etc., but simply with telling a story, any story. No wonder Froebel was not prepared to separate his theory from his practice when urged to do so. No wonder he always maintained that his play activities, games and occupations would only escape thoughtless usage if the reasons behind each activity were fully understood.

Probably the most striking impression which remains with us after reading the Mother Songs, is that of Froebel's vision of a unifying, integrating and continuing method of education which allows him to present to us the total picture as well as the final aims, illustrating how the very young child's earliest physical movements will eventually lead to abstract thinking.

In his introduction to the Mother Songs, Froebel starts off by reminding the mother, that the new-born child has to be seen as a gift of the 'Father of all Creation', revealing His very nature in the child, and thus confronting us with a complete and 'unified being'. Froebel now encourages the mother to observe her child carefully and to notice his individuality and his characteristics, as well as the completeness of his being. Observations will show that the child's senses as well as his movements of body and limbs are all concentrating on achieving one goal, namely to experience life in its details in order to understand its totality. The child will do this, so mothers will observe, by expressing what the child feels and knows, and also by his wish to 'absorb the external so as to re-create it from within'. Mother's aim in life must be to educate her child in such a way that he can achieve this final goal of 'unity'.

But *how* can it be achieved?

> How else . . . than through the body, limbs and senses, . . . by his paying attention and by his own efforts; how else than by his relationship with you (Mother) and others; how else, than by the awareness of his gradually awakening mind.[20]

These are the characteristics which will lead to the child's autonomy and mother has to 'wait for, foster and develop' these characteristics.

Each song and play activity may be structured from without, but Froebel leaves us in no doubt as to the only possible way in which he believes the educational process has to proceed. He demonstrates convincingly by his reminder to mothers that they are dealing with a unique being - a being with his own characteristics and his own individuality, a being who strives to live and learn and comprehend - as well as by his reminder that comprehension depends, in the first place, on the learner's own actions and 'his paying attention', internalising information and re-creating it is his own special way, that his Mother Songs could never be considered as an instrument for learning without freedom being granted.

It is significant that Froebel does not once refer to 'free play' in the Mother Songs, his last major creative work. His belief about how young children learn left Froebel in no doubt as to how they had to be taught. The child's physical and mental ability and his interests provided the carefully observing teacher with the clue as to what and how to teach. Such observations could never be made without a child's freedom to indicate to the educator which lines to follow and what procedure to adopt in order to achieve his educational goal. It was too obvious to be stated.

1. Seele, nd, MS 33/142-178, p.143.
2. ibid.
3. Froebel *in* Pruefer, 1927, p.1.
4. Froebel *in* Seidel, vol III, 1883, p.124.
5. Piaget, 1953, p.142.
6. ibid, p.155.
7. ibid, p.143.
8. Flavell, 1963, p.159.
9. Inhelder & Piaget, 1964, p.291.
10. Heiland, 1967, p.8.
11. King, 1970, p.39.
12. Froebel *in* Bollnow, 1967, p.205.
13. Robinson, 1972, p.68.
14. Froebel *in* Seidel, vol III, 1883, p.182.
15. Froebel, 1842, MS 8/47/29-94, p.84.
16. Froebel *in* Seidel, vol III, 1883, p.158.
17. Stead, 1905, p.46.
18. ibid, p.36.
19. ibid, p.5.
20. Froebel *in* Seidel, vol III, 1883, p.121.

# Chapter 8
# Criticisms of Froebel's Work, Then and Now

Thunder and lightning forced children and parents, friends and relations, teachers and headmasters, present pupils and past scholars who followed Froebel's coffin to the tiny churchyard in Schweina, to look for shelter. 'Even his last journey passes through wind and storm,' commented the parson who was walking beside Middendorff, and not until the coffin had been lowered into the ground did the sun give its approval.[1] Froebel, no doubt, would have seen in it a fitting and truly symbolic ending to his life.

Official censure by governments and continuous criticism by individuals can be traced from Froebel's earliest endeavours in Keilhau to the 'Kindergarten Verbot' in August 1851, in his last year of life. He was accused of being an atheist and egotist, of being simple-minded, of misleading the young and of preaching revolution. His Gifts were considered to be too simple for children to play with and at the same time too difficult for teachers to understand, his methods to be irrational and too mechanical, the symbolism used too fanciful and the Kindergarten a questionable institution. Some of these criticisms, often with a different emphasis, are again under discussion today. It is proposed to deal with the criticisms of Froebel's contemporaries in the first part of this chapter, to compare them with those of present-day writers and to provide answers and clarifications, based on the manuscripts used in this book, towards the end of this chapter.

All the criticisms levelled against Froebel in his life-time can be grouped into criticisms of his person, criticisms of his methods and criticisms of his philosophy. Although his contemporaries very often combine one area of criticism with another, especially as regards to method and philosophy, it may prove helpful to separate these areas whenever possible.

Marenholtz-Bülow's reminiscences of Froebel as a person portray him as an idealist, unselfish and totally dedicated to the welfare of children. Yet people also believed Froebel to be 'an egotist who knew everything best'[2] and a man who showed little tolerance to those who disagreed with him even when they were his most trusted friends.

On one occasion, Middendorff experienced Froebel's wrath when executing some games with the children in a manner of which Froebel did not approve. The reprimand which followed took place in front of the children and the students, 'who were most surprised, secretly considered it to be a pedagogical mistake to behave in such a manner.'[3]

Froebel was aware of this shortcoming of his, at least in the early days in Keilhau, and questioned the rationality of his behaviour, for it was contrary to his own philosophy. A diary entry of 1821 reads as follows:

> It is highly remarkable how every encounter which represents a slanted opinion, e.g. as with Langethal, excites and irritates me. How each personal, especially individual opinion which to me does not relate to the whole, can put me into a highly excited state and irritate me. (As, for example, Langethal's opinion relating to language and music.) Why should this be so? - Is it not better to let everybody go his own way? Everybody must develop in his own way, for everybody has to follow the path which God has given.[4]

Froebel's disagreements with the Keilhau families, shortly before he left for Switzerland, are well known. However practical Froebel's approach to the education of young children, there was no realistic approach to the financial side of his ventures. Though pupils and staff might already be short of food and clothing, Froebel would not think twice of coming back with yet another stray child to be cared for. The ensuing argument about finance only convinced Froebel that 'they' did not really understand him. Froebel's rift with the women in these difficult days in Keilhau seems to have been greater than with the men. But then the material care of the community rested in the women's hands and in addition, it also affected their own children.

> With the exception of Middendorff, no one speaks cordially of him (Froebel). In Rudolstadt he is not given recognition in the same way as are Barop, Middendorff, uncle and aunt. These call Froebel impractical and an idealist and consider it good fortune that he has retired from the institution . . . . They say that he constantly borrowed money for his work, and when the uncle would no longer help him in this way, Froebel was angry with him . . . .[5]

Material wealth had no meaning to Froebel unless it was used to the betterment of mankind. It would be wrong to assume that this referred to his educational ideas and plans only. When some peasants from the neighbouring village knocked at his door begging for food and money because their house had been burnt down, Froebel, being without money as usual, emptied his wardrobe of its content and gave that away. Froebel's egotism related to his ideas and not to his person, especially as he never considered these ideas to be his own, but himself only the mouthpiece of what had to be by necessity.

Criticisms of his methods gathered momentum over the years. The most serious attacks were made at the teachers' conference in Rudolstadt (17-19 August 1848), which Froebel himself had called in order to demonstrate the play activities in his Kindergarten and to explain the philosophical and educational reasons underlying them.[6] To assess the validity of these criticisms, it is important to realize that by 1848, eight years after Froebel had opened his first Kindergarten, a considerable number of people from different walks of life had come to see Froebel's work and had heard about it from lectures and demonstrations given by Froebel all over Germany.

Far from being an idealist living in an ivory tower Froebel had realized that the formation of Kindergartens all over the country would depend largely on three groups of people: the aristocracy, who might provide land, building and finance as well as popularise the idea by showing interest; the writers, philosophers, artists, printers and editors, who would discuss the ideas and disseminate information; and finally the practising educators who had to be convinced of the validity of his claims and its relevance in the classroom.

In Thuringia, the mother of the reigning Duke of Schwarzburg-Rudolstadt as well as the Princess Carolina Ida von Schaumburg-Lippe were showing considerable interest in Froebel's work as early as 1840, while the lecture which Froebel gave in 1839 in Dresden was attended by the Queen of Saxony, the principal of Dresden's polytechnic, the headmaster of the Dresden Grammar School, medical doctors, local poets, artists, sculptors, physicians, theologians and high-ranking civil servants of the King's Government.[7]

On his journey through Western Germany in 1844, Froebel also lectured in Cologne and was promised support by the editor of the *Koelner Zeitung*, a paper with one of the largest circulations in Germany at the time. In Wiesbaden the philosopher Schliephake met Froebel for the first and probably only time. Yet it was a meeting which impressed Schliephake, for many years later he read a paper to the Philosophers' Congress in Frankfurt (1869) on 'Froebel's Educational Principles' in which he assessed Froebel's ideas favourably.

Dr Foelsing, one of Froebel's critics at the Rudolstadt Conference, though not personally present at the conference, had taken time and trouble to write a lengthy paper about his experiences with Froebel's Gifts, which was presented to the large gathering. Foelsing, a practising teacher who had founded a private school for pre-school-age children in 1843, was also the most prolific and most successful writer on pre-school education at the time. His writings were more widely known and understood than those of Froebel. Froebel visited Foelsing and their common interests and aims created a friendship which lasted till Froebel's death, even though the two men disagreed on the methods to be used.

By the time the Rudolstadt Conference took place, Froebel's work was widely known even if not well understood. Teachers, headteachers, inspectors and others interested in pre-school education attended the conference. There were those who criticised from partial ignorance, among them Kell, the editor of the *Lehrer-Zeitung* in Leipzig. Then there were the critics who considered Froebel's ideas and methods far too revolutionary and unworkable in the classroom and finally, and in a way unexpectedly, those who expressed concern that Froebel's ideas were not progressive enough.[8] Hanschmann's judgement[9] that the conference above all criticised Froebel's methods because 'children's play activities in the Kindergarten made work in later school life more difficult' is not born out by the Conference Report. True, the criticisms levelled against Froebel's work, were substantial yet at the end of this three day debate the conference passed a resolution to recommend the establishment of Froebelian Kindergartens to the German National Assembly which was just then meeting in Frankfurt.

Most participants of the Rudolstadt Conference were impressed with the children's activities demonstrated on the first day, but doubts were expressed as to their suitability for general use. Even if children could survive such rigorous activities day after day, surely the teacher could not. It would be far too difficult to maintain such a pace in an ordinary Kindergarten. It was also not clear to the members of the conference whether what they had witnessed the children doing was supposed to be play or work. Some maintained that too little teaching had been going on during these activities while others maintained that too much had been done.[10] 'Learning playfully' was an extraordinary idea, as Foelsing pointed out especially as everybody knew that a child had to 'play out' his childhood. To learn while playing was a contradiction of the word 'play' as Foelsing understood it.[11]

Yet many teachers would not agree with that interpretation of play either. The last teachers' conference which Froebel attended in his life-time (Liebenstein, September 1851) emphasised that if play did not lead to 'serious activity, it was one-sided'. There had been criticism that children who had gone through a Froebel Kindergarten and were used to the play-activities were reluctant to settle down to serious work when they entered Elementary School,[12] though there were those, who testified to the contrary and found such children 'obedient, friendly and alert', but they had the fault of asking too many questions which it was not possible to answer with a hundred children in the class.[13]

Most teachers at the conference could see the usefulness of the Gifts and Games as a means of keeping children happily occupied, but they had little understanding of and patience with Froebel's theories. The whole system, with its frequent references to fractions as well as geometrical shapes was considered too mathematical and would therefore not be understood by the elementary school teachers who would have to use it. One would have to separate the theory from the practice and suggestions were made to Froebel that he should write a comprehensive account of all the possible activities, occupations and games for the use of teachers in schools.[14] There were also those who could not see the point of using sticks or cubes as play materials anyway. The whole system was not rational.

The Gifts were also criticised on the grounds that they were too structured and therefore unsuitable for easy usage and adaptation by the children. The third Gift, consisting of eight cubes, was too limiting, while the division of the cube in the fifth Gift consisting of twenty-seven smaller cubes was too difficult for children under the age of six. Other subdivisions, apart from the fourth Gift, should have been made between the two. The intellectual jump demanded from the children was too great to be made successfully.[15] The usage of these Gifts also limited the child's development of fantasy especially as Froebel did not include fairy-stories in his occupations. The games and the rhymes which were suggested were 'of little use in later life'.[16]

Foelsing who had tried out Froebel's Gifts in his own school made similar criticisms in a paper which he had sent to the conference for distribution. He also expressed misgivings about the ages of the children for whom the Gifts were designed. Foelsing believed, that Froebel was expecting too much from the children at too early an age. Foelsing observed children at their straw and paper weaving and only three out of ten 5-6 year-olds succeeded in some measure. Most of it had to be done by the teacher.

Yet in the report of the opening of the first Kindergarten in Frankfurt, we hear that an 'influential family' withdrew their eldest daughter from the Kindergarten after three days attendance, 'because she was soon going to be six'.[17] As her two younger sisters remained at the Kindergarten, we may assume that the reason for withdrawal was to be found in the parents' estimation of suitability for this particular age, rather than in a general criticism.

Froebel's philosophy was attacked in general terms as being too difficult to understand and therefore of little value to the practising schoolmaster, but also because some of its implications ran contrary to contemporary beliefs and practices, especially as regards to moral and religious education.

During the Rudolstadt Conference Froebel was pressed once again, as on many previous and later occasions, to separate his theory from his Gifts, Games and Occupations. Whenever Froebel explained the Gifts and Occupations, he would always link the *how* with the *why*. But the *why*, because it included philosophy, theology, mathematics, psychology and biology, was so complex, that it could never be explained successfully in a series of lectures, let alone at one conference or during one conversation. Even his students at Marienthal who attended his courses for at least six months seemed to be at a loss at times - especially when Froebel lectured about the very young child and his inability to comprehend, and how therefore the first objects for play must be carefully selected to present 'symbolically' the reality and truth of life. When coloured balls were made to represent the rainbow spectrum which in turn was interpreted as the symbol of peace between God and man, Froebel became an easy target for ridicule and misunderstanding.

A more ordinary and less imaginative man, and one less firmly held by a vulnerable philosophy might have seen the ridiculous artificiality and unnecessary complexity of some Froebelian material.[18]

No wonder that students' notebooks, which Froebel frequently collected after lectures, were often a source of sorrow to him when they betrayed once more that he had not been understood. Yet to provide the materials for play without the reasons behind each activity was unthinkable to Froebel. He always maintained that his material did not contain anything new, children had always played with balls and bricks, nor was its virtue to be seen in its external appearance, for it was of the greatest simplicity. Indeed, that was precisely its virtue. Its value was to be found in the way in which it was used, its method, and the method depended on the natural law of unity, ultimately the unity with God.

A substantial part of the criticism levelled against Froebel's philosophy related to his religious ideas. The charge that Froebel was an atheist was of long standing. Froebel mentioned attacks of this kind as far back as 1840, (in a letter to Friederika Schmidt, dated 12 September 1840). They probably originated from Froebel's refusal to tolerate the teaching of church dogma in his Kindergarten. But this refusal was again based on his philosophy of the nature of man and his knowledge of children. It was part of the system. Religion was not a matter of church going and beliefs in dogma but of personal relationships. 'When child and parents grow up together in harmony . . . they have laid the foundation stone for true religion.'[19]

The love of God could not be demonstrated except through the love of man. Families where parents loved and respected their children were fulfilling 'the prayer of Christ'. These relationships of love and respect were also essential in the classroom. Without this foundation the teaching of religion was fraught with dangers and pitfalls. No wonder so much religious teaching had to be underpinned with the threat of hell-fire and the reward in heaven for the good deeds done on earth. Yet were not both these a degradation of the spirit of man and of God?

Judging from all accounts it is almost certain that Froebel did not take 'prayers' with the children in his Kindergarten, but he also did not object when others did. We have an account by one of his Kindergarten teachers about Froebel's unexpected visit to the Kindergarten early in the morning, when she was in the middle of morning prayers with the children. Froebel was obviously moved by the simplicity and sincerity of the occasion and at the conclusion of prayers said:

A mother should and can pray with young children, and you are their mother at the moment. A man, a father, cannot talk to the children like this, cannot pray with the children in such a way.[20]

There were also criticisms of the Kindergarten as an institution. Froebel's critics maintained that a Kindergarten was educationally unsound because the best place for a young child's education was his home. It was right to provide Kindergartens for the poor, but there was no need to do the same for the children of the well-to-do. Indeed, this would be harmful, as no Kindergarten teacher could provide the love of a mother which the child would receive at home. Therefore, Kindergartens must never be made compulsory like schools. At any rate, it would not be possible to find enough Kindergarten teachers, for it was well known, they maintained, that women are only capable of a limited amount of education, and Froebel's system based on philosophical arguments was completely out of range of women's understanding.[21]

A few institutions which looked after pre-school-age children were already in existence in the middle of the last century, but these were places where children could be 'left' rather than where children could play. A visitor to such an institution wrote at the time:

the play material consisted of four wooden blocks, the size of table legs. That was all (apart from four to six slates for drawing) that this institution possessed. I encouraged the supervisor to carry out some movement play with the children, but she had scarcely the energy to get the children off the sand floor into a circle.[22]

The need for these institutions arose because parents, having to work all day, had to leave their children who did not go to school, either roaming the streets or locked up in the house. One of the early Kindergarten teachers writing to Froebel about her work, tells him how on her way to the Kindergarten each morning, she lifted children out of their homes through the windows because the doors were locked, and then took the children with her to the Kindergarten. The child-minding institution in Darmstadt came into existence after three children had been burnt to death in their home, while their parents were working in the fields.[23]

Froebel's demand for the establishment of Kindergartens in every town and village therefore met with sympathy in some quarters. Yet Froebel's Kindergarten differed essentially from the existing institutions, *Bewahranstalten*, as regards the treatment of the children who attended. While child-minding institutions simply made sure that children were fed during the day and came to no harm, Froebel considered pre-school education an essential part of the total educational process. The Kindergarten was 'the mediator between child, family and society'. Froebel therefore considered it essential that all children - not only those of the poor - should have the opportunity to attend the Kindergarten.

The criticism by royal courts and governments, of the Kindergarten as an institution, is of a different order. The introduction of the 'People's Kindergarten' in Dresden did not please the Queen of Saxony: 'To educate the common people is just about the end. Probably it will then become even more difficult to govern them.'[24]

The same kind of fear must have been the basis for the Kindergarten Verbot of 1851 which closed all Kindergartens in the country. It is clear from the Verbot itself, that Froebel had been mistaken for his nephew Karl whose papers 'High School and Kindergarten' were cited in the Verbot as socialistic and atheistic. Even after the mistake had been pointed out to the Minister, he still maintained that Froebel's 'theory of education ran contrary to Christian belief'.[25] Socialism and atheism were synonymous with lawlessness and revolution and there were plenty of signs that the 1848 revolution might spread to Vienna and Berlin. To support ideas which advocated freedom in any form whatsoever, was playing into the hands of those who demanded constitutional changes. They therefore had to be silenced.

It seems ironic that the educator who always insisted that every construction made in the classroom must never be destroyed but used as a basis for the following construction, whose whole system was based on 'education by development', should be thought of as a destructive revolutionary; that the idealist whose philosophy was 'unity and harmony' and whose ultimate desire was to bring mankind to the realization of 'unity with God', should be labelled an atheist; and that the man who recognised law and order in every flower, every stone and every action and made this the basis for his teaching, should be feared in case his influence should lead to lawlessness and destruction. The Government Verbot had the unfortunate effect of ensuring that the Kindergarten issue was now taken up by several political parties, especially the radicals who, in so doing, hoped to gain support for their own cause.

Yet even those who were apparently able to appreciate the value of Froebel's venture into pre-school education found something to criticise. They seemed to approve of what Froebel had done, but wanted to know why he had not continued the system to include children and young people up to the age of eighteen or twenty. What about the teaching of foreign languages and at what age should they be started? Which poets ought to be taught and in what order? How far should tradition play a part in education? Froebel answered by saying he wished people would not ask him questions which they themselves were better qualified to answer than he.

Except for Froebel's letters to the Prussian Minister of Education, von Raumer, and his letter to the King of Prussia requesting the authorities to examine his methods and to reconsider their Kindergarten Verbot, Froebel never justified his work in writing, for the benefit of his critics, though frequently encouraged by his friends to do so. He always maintained, that if his educational ideas and methods were true and correct, they would stand the test of time and no justification was necessary; if not, they would not be worth defending. In a debate he would pay no heed to personal attacks, though he would vehemently defend his ideas and ideals.

After Froebel's death and towards the turn of the century the major criticisms were directed against the use of the Gifts and the Occupations. Teachers who had instructed their children with the help of the Kindergarten apparatus with too much enthusiasm and too little imagination found themselves under attack for occupying children with meaningless tasks. The drawing and stick-laying exercises, the bead-threading occupations and the cutting-out and weaving exercises, all lend themselves to misuse by thoughtless teachers. The drawing exercises were frequently quoted as an illustration to demonstrate the shortcomings of some of Froebel's methods.

In his instructions Froebel starts off by encouraging teachers to reflect on children's interest in pictures which, Froebel believes, leads to scribbling as an appropriate activity for a child who is not yet able to express his 'inner life' in any other form. The child then asks adults to draw him 'a cat', 'a bird', etc. and finally attempts to do it himself.

Froebel then provides the child with squared paper which will aid his efforts 'as it does a draughtsman'. Vertical and horizontal lines are drawn, triangles and squares, the 'law of opposites' is brought into operation to demonstrate the reverse of each figure and so children progress to drawing flowers, houses and animals. It is all governed by straight lines and their connections, the point and the circle.

To follow such instructions slavishly deserves, no doubt, severe criticism. Yet, teachers who see little value in drawing and belittle children's efforts quite clearly do not appreciate the link between drawing and the cognitive value of representation. Froebel, too, may not have understood the psychological processes involved in detail, but he must have surmised them when he wrote:

. . . as long as we do not recognise drawing as an essential part of the educational process, we are depriving man of one of the most effective means of education.[26]

If we compare the criticism levelled against Froebel's educational theory and practice by his contemporaries with those by present-day writers, we find considerable differences.

While Froebel's contemporaries criticised his philosophy on the grounds that it was too difficult to understand and also because it ran contrary to contemporary beliefs, especially as regards moral and religious education, present-day writers criticise his philosophy because it produces a theory of education which takes its model from plants and non-organic matter. The growth-theory of education is found deficient. Froebel's contemporaries also did not advance many criticisms as regards the role of the teacher, yet it greatly disturbs present-day writers. To them it looks as if Froebel's teachers have abdicated all responsibility in the classroom, leaving children to get on with their own learning. This, of course, leads to the criticism that Froebel concentrated too much on the education of the individual and left out the social aspect of learning. The Kindergarten as an educational institution is no longer questioned, only Froebel's theory of play is under attack as before. Today, as 150 years ago, it is criticised by some because it allows too much freedom and lacks direction, while others believe that it is too structured and prevents creativity.

Looking at today's critics in more detail, we can do no better than to take Dearden as our guide. He starts off by pointing out the shortcomings of the growth theory and shows how it leads inevitably to a discussion of the role of the teacher and the examination of the function of freedom and play in Froebel's education.

Dearden points out that Froebel's theory, based on nature, suffers from the assumption that what is 'natural' in the unfolding is right and ignores the social aspect in human development. As the development of children takes place in a social setting, it is quite unlike the unfolding of a plant. Because 'Froebel explicitly likened education to the biological unfolding of inner potentialities,'[27] it was bound to change teacher-directed education to a system where the inner, hidden potentials of the child were bound to be given more importance than the 'external or manifest'. In consequence, so Dearden maintains, the teacher's role is reduced to that of an observer or at best to a gardener, tending his plants.

Dearden is not alone in drawing such a conclusion. Cyril Burt, quoting Froebel's saying that 'young as he is, each child unconsciously knows and wills what is best for him,' believes that earlier pioneers of child-centred education, like Froebel, would have heartily endorsed the aphorisms of today's 'progressives' that a teacher should never say 'no'.[28]

We notice that Froebel's critics are above all concerned with the measure of how much freedom and how much direction is essential, or desirable, for educational processes to take their course. Traditional education is then often compared with child-centred education and a third alternative is suggested. Dearden again provides us with an example of such an argument.

In his article on 'Instruction and Learning by Discovery' Dearden introduces the topic by differentiating between the elementary school tradition and the developmental tradition where the 'latter is especially associated with Froebel and those theories often referred to as "child-centred" '.[29]

Dearden first considers carefully the appropriateness of instruction as a means for teaching and comes to the conclusion that in many instances this may be the most economical and successful way for the teacher to achieve his goal, especially when learning processes involve the acquisition of skills as in swimming, carpentry, reading, handwriting or French. But he believes that knowledge which requires the operational mastery of concepts and principles, as in mathematics, science and history, would require more than instruction.

He now turns to the discussion of 'learning by discovery' and taking the pre-school model as his example, expresses his grave doubts as to the educational value of haphazard investigations and discoveries when children are pottering about. Even when teachers present materials which are so structured that children supposedly cannot help but learn from it, Dearden quite rightly points out, the abstractions children may make from such material may be quite different from those which the teacher hoped they would make.

In his concluding pages, Dearden provides us with the solution by suggesting that discovery methods need explaining, probing and questioning by the teacher. He states:

> 'Learning by Discovery' can be given another, and much more plausible, interpretation besides the interpretation, based on the model of pre-school learning or abstractionism.[30]

In this third model, Dearden suggests, the teacher is not just a provider of material from which the child supposedly abstracts what the teacher desires him to know, but one who 'discusses, instructs, hints, questions and suggests' what to do in order to find out. Dearden believes that this third method of learning by discovery has to be set 'in the strongest possible contrast to the interpretations based on pre-school-learning and abstractionism . . . .'[31] because it does not 'provide experience, but guides experience' by the use of language towards something which is educationally worthwhile achieving. The crucial role of language in concept formation as well as the importance of the teacher as the guiding and intervening agent are stressed. Because discovery methods are linked with 'child-centred education' and 'pre-school education', and all these with Froebel, the implications are that Froebel did not clarify his position as regards the role of the teacher and paid little or no attention to the importance of language.

Dearden's belief that the teacher had little or no function in Froebel's education, is also evident in his chapter on 'Play' where he leaves us in no doubt that Froebel's children grew into adults without help or hindrance of any kind. Dearden believes that play could only be considered educational if the activities were so arranged that they would give evidence of a continuous development which would give cognitive perspective to one's experience, and that such activities would have to be in line with what is to be achieved in later schooling. 'The adults who supervise such play would indeed be teachers and would also have arranged an educational situation.'[32] In his assessment Froebel's ideas on play do not meet these requirements.

However there are those who criticise Froebel's theory of play for exactly the opposite reasons. To them, Froebelian play was not educative because it was hampered by too many directions, it was too formal. Brubacher supports Froebel's growth theory. He says:'Nothing can unfold from seed or cell which was not unfolded in inception. This is the lesson of Froebel's Kindergarten.'[33] But when he comes to assess the Kindergarten play, he considers it to be too formal, not allowing the child enough freedom for experimentation.

Similarly, Morrish[34] states that to present play material in Froebel's fashion, directing and controlling it, and to insist that it was educative and purposive, was to reduce play to a 'drill' which children certainly could not enjoy. Such formalised play, whatever the theory behind it, Morrish maintains, could never be educative because it lacked spontaneity.

The new perspective gained from this study of the original manuscripts used in this book regarding Froebel's theory of play, his ideas about children's freedom for active participation in the learning process and above all the role of the educator in all this, should help to diminish the most obvious present-day misconceptions about Froebel's intentions and indeed his practice.

Froebel's 'growth-theory' is probably responsible for the major part of today's criticisms of his ideas on education. The quotations used by Dearden, Burt, Brubacher and others are all taken from *The Education of Man*, published in 1826, at a time when Froebel had barely started his career as an educator. The most burning issue at this time, as far as Froebel was concerned, was to free children from the drudgery of rote-learning whenever possible. At the same time he wanted adults to be more aware of children's sensitivity during their most formative years. The adult world which he was addressing in his book was predominantly agricultural by origin and occupation. What better way than to use the plant metaphor to make people see and understand.

It is perfectly true that Froebel believed in the innate goodness of man and that, if conditions were right, goodness would prevail. But this did not mean that he was not aware of the shortcomings of man, or children for that matter. In one of his many drafts relating to the first Gift he says:

> The play medium must not awaken too quickly nor forcefully the animal instincts, the low and the sensuous, which are linked with human nature and is present in the child in the form of impatience, aping and greed.[35]

Froebel is also aware that such instincts will have already been awakened in children 'unavoidably' before they come to school and therefore educators had to be careful not to provide play material for the children which might 'nourish' these undesirable traits. Whenever children did behave in an unacceptable manner, as for example in the Blankenburg Kindergarten where children were found stealing, Froebel would not condone such actions but would alter the situation so that the opportunity for wrong-doing was minimised.

The criticism that Froebel's comparison of children with growing plants did not take account of man's social nature is only valid as long as one ignores the rest of Froebel's teaching on the upbringing of children. A study of his writings reveals above all Froebel's belief in the 'unity of all things', where the child is firmly placed in the family setting, the family in the village, the village in the larger context of the country and finally mankind in general. In the Kindergarten children were encouraged to work with each other because they could learn from each other. Models built by one child might lead to discussion and give others inspiration for improvements. But even the Movement Games which Froebel especially designed for children's greater freedom to express their ideas and inclinations - in contrast to the Gifts where the structuring was external - emphasise the social aspect of children's lives. Very rarely are these games mentioned in publications about Froebel, and several of the games devised by Froebel were never published. As outlined in this book, their study reveals a careful progression from the Wander Games where the individual child is free to wander where he likes, and visit whom he likes, to games which involve two and three children, culminating in Circle Games where other children's wishes and demands have to be taken into consideration. Above all, the reports written by Froebel's ex-pupils leave us in no doubt about the social character of the Keilhau community where children contributed by their own efforts in the garden and in the fields, in the kitchen and the sewing-room, the workshop and the stables, to the well-being of all.

The most serious criticism, however, and probably also the most justifiable one judging by what Froebel had said in *The Education of Man*, relates to the role of the teacher. Froebel's concern about adults' insensitive behaviour towards children, whether in school, in the family or in society in general, led him to assign a different role to the teacher as commonly understood. Froebel's frequently quoted passage that educators must in the first instance 'be passive, observing and following', together with Froebel's notion of the 'unfolding child', was taken to mean that the teacher had now become a benevolent child-minder, allowing children freedom for expression, refraining from all interferences in children's play activities, no longer planning their learning and indeed reluctant to say 'no', even when educational considerations or common-sense dictated otherwise.

In fairness to Froebel it must be pointed out, that even in *The Education of Man*, he qualified his statement about the passive and following teacher by saying that he must be both: 'dictating and following, acting and enduring, deciding and freedom allowing, firm and flexible. Yet the notion of the 'following teacher' was so alien to the generations of educators to come, that it is not surprising that they should have concentrated on this new aspect of the role of the teacher and should have ignored the qualifications. Froebel's concept of the role of the teacher is, of course, closely related to his ideas about freedom in education. The original manuscripts used here shed considerable light on both concepts.

Originally, Froebel planned his Gifts to function 'auto-didactically'. It was his intention to develop toys which would be self-educative, and the first cube he constructed served the purpose of teaching geometry. It reflects Froebel's earlier emphasis on the role of the teacher as the provider of the right kind of environment. But this direct teaching through the cube, which now became the teacher, was only possible if the child was able to read, thus it was limited to children of school age. To construct a cube which was truly self-educative would be so complex as to render it probably incomprehensible. Another solution would be to give a wider and deeper meaning to his activities by the means of the use of language. The mother will explain the characteristics and functions of the Gifts, but even in the guide-lines to the first Gift we find that the child must hold and play with the ball himself. The explanations to the third Gift, especially the 1844 version, demonstrate the integration between the child's spontaneity and the adult's guidance most successfully. At first, the child's joy in exploration and discovery must dominate his activity. Then the adult moves into the child's sphere of activity and thinking, and extends and deepens his play through the explanatory word. The emphasis is not on instruction but on active participation in a child's play which aims at maintaining interest and deepening the understanding of what the child vaguely surmises.

By this process Froebel is able to maintain the essential characteristics of play as outlined in Chapter Three and yet use it for educational purposes. The measure of freedom lost when the adult enters into a child's play activities will vary from person to person. As long as the adult is aware of the problem, and sensitive towards its solution, Froebel was convinced that learning could progress without play having to cease.

Freedom, to Froebel, was never a goal to be achieved, for it was inexhaustible, each consequence demanding a new choice be made. Nor was it an ideal to be pursued for its own sake, but a potential for action, for 'creative thinking' within the framework of play. Judging Froebel by his actions, and especially referring to the little known incident where he wanted to try out his Gifts for the first time with a child from his school, we can safely say that he himself not only believed in, but also practised an education of which 'rational freedom' was an essential part. No longer can the role of the educator be seen in terms of the teacher as commonly understood, nor in terms of the gardener of Froebel's earlier vision who provided and allowed growth to take its course, but as a guide and mentor who by his participation in a child's play gives meaning and depth and breadth to a child's activities.

There is one other area which needs our attention, especially in consideration of Piaget's evaluation of Froebel's educational theory and practice - an area which is closely related to play and the concept of freedom, namely that of the child's own action in the learning process.

Piaget mentions that Froebel's education, like Pestalozzi's, was primarily based on sense-training.[36] He argues that the 'seven famous Occupations', though encouraging activity also falsify the idea of activity by preventing genuine creativity. Piaget believes that a radical change in the understanding of children's learning did not come about until the early twentieth century, when it was realized that the 'life of the mind' could not be explained by static elements like receptivity and retention but by analysis of activity and the processes of ongoing mental constructions.

It is difficult to see which criteria Piaget could have used to come to the conclusion that Pestalozzi's, let alone Froebel's, methods of education are based on 'sense-training'. True, Pestalozzi's greatest innovation in educational practice, learning by careful observation of the real object, is partly based on 'seeing and perceiving', but reflection - that is structuring of what had been seen, was a large part of his method. And the vital difference between Pestalozzi's *Anschauungs-Unterricht* based on deductions gained from visual observations as compared with Froebel's activity methods, where learning was based on reflection on actions, have been dealt with in detail in this book. Equally so the creative aspects in Froebel's play theory.

But it seems important, in view of Piaget's statement that the function of activity in the learning process was not appreciated until the twentieth century, to focus once more on Froebel's understanding and explanations of the value of activity to the learner. Froebel believed that knowledge and activity were of equal importance because knowledge depended on reflection, and reflection on man's own actions.[37] The learner had to be actively involved, had to focus on his actions and reflect upon them before learning could take place. True, Froebel did not talk of 'mental structures building up', but he encouraged mothers (and teachers) to involve children in similar activities several times over because he believed that once a child had made two separate observations, he would be put into the position where he could 'deduce' (or structure) the third and following ones for himself. These transformational mental activities are further emphasised by Froebel in his 'Simple Educational and Developmental Laws of the Child'[38] where he deals with the creative aspect of imitation and where he states that imitation in its most elementary aspects demands a 're-presentation from within by an unfamiliar action'. Even if we cannot credit Froebel with seeing the mind as a dynamic intelligence as envisaged by Bergson, Binet or Wundt in the twentieth century, we can certainly observe that to Froebel the human mind was an active participant in the learning process which had to reorganise incoming information, to deduce, discard and recreate - and not a passive agent for receiving information and storing knowledge, as generally believed in the nineteenth century.

It is probably not surprising that the ideas for which Froebel has been attacked most severely are also the ideas which have had the greatest influence on our educational thinking and practices during the last hundred years. At first these influences were limited to the treatment of the pre-school child, but because they were so fundamental and embraced universal truths applicable to children of any age, they soon affected the work in the primary schools and have now entered the secondary school field. What, in summary, are these ideas? If, as has been suggested, it is true that much of this theory is now common practice in our schools, what is worth restating for the 1990s?

1. Kuntze, 1952, p.136.
2. Seele, nd, MS 33/142-178, p.178.
3. ibid, p.149.
4. Froebel, 1821, MS 17, p.146.
5. Caxton, 1914, p.161.
6. Conference Report, 1848, MS 7/43/76-97.
7. Hanschmann, 1875, p.301.
8. Conference Report, 1848, MS 7/43/76-97.
9. Hanschmann, 1875, p.355.
10. Conference Report, 1848, MS 7/43/76-97, p.47, p.91.
11. Foelsing, 1848, MS 7/42/25-29.
12. Conference Report, 1851, MS 21/22/1.
13. Seele, nd, MS 33/142-178, p.170.
14. Conference Report, 1848, MS 7/43/76-97, p.86.
15. Seele, nd, MS 33/142-178.
16. ibid, p.177.
17. Report on the Opening of a Kindergarten, 1839, MS 21/20/0.
18. Castle, 1970, p.131.
19. Froebel *in* Lange, 1863, p.190.
20. Seele, nd, MS 33/142-178, p.168.
21. Conference Report, 1848, MS 7/43/76-97.
22. Schuffenhauer, 1962, p.58.
23. Seele, nd, MS 33/142-178, p.159.
24. Kuntze, 1952, p.129.
25. Hanschmann, 1875, p.423.
26. Froebel, 1830, MS 19/9/5/159-160.
27. Dearden, Hirst & Peters, 1972, p.66.
28. Cox & Dyson, nd, p.16.
29. Peters, 1967, p.147.
30. ibid, p.150.
31. ibid, p.151.
32. ibid, p.78.
33. Brubacher, 1969, p.140.
34. Morrish, 1970, p.204.
35. Froebel, 1840, MS 18/5/1/1-57.
36. Piaget, 1970, p.9, p.34, p.97.
37. Froebel, 1838, 18ab. 4/F.5.
38. Froebel, 1845, MS 19/8/5/122-127.

# Chapter 9
# Froebel's Greatest Contributions to Educational Thinking

Froebel's greatest contributions to educational thinking are to be found in the area of how children learn. Froebel puts before us the idea that a child's intellectual development begins on the day he is born. This, inevitably, makes the mother the child's first teacher, and Froebel makes us aware that 'mother-love' by itself will not be sufficient to do the job successfully. As the child, at this state in his life, has only his own actions available by which to learn, Froebel argues that the child's actions are the seed kernel of his intelligence. This individual activity, although demonstrating what is within the child, his gifts and interests, needs encouragement from without and with the help of the adult, self-activity changes into play. Play now becomes the instrument for learning because it provides the ideal situation for awareness of the self, the outside world and the interaction of the two. With increased intelligence the child needs to reflect on his experiences and therefore needs to represent his own thinking in terms of actions and language.

As this is the most important learning period in a child's life, it cannot be left to busy parents alone. It needs the support of the trained expert in a specially built institution, a Kindergarten, as well as the support provided by the interaction with other children. Because such an expert is aware that children have to do their own learning, she knows that the role of the teacher is no longer that of an instructor, but that of a facilitator and guide.

Froebel's observations of children showed him that young children's thinking does not proceed by logical concepts but by a process of reasoning from the particular to the particular. Much has to be done by having hunches, much has to be surmised. This, of course, is also what grown-ups have to do in many of their adult activities. They too are not capable of solving all their problems by logical steps. The fostering of the surmise and the use of the symbol became an important aspect of Froebel's education. It is an area which is not yet part of present-day educational thinking and which will need our attention in the 1990s. But some of the other principles too need restating at a time when the shift is, once more, towards the more formal, the more restrictive and less creative mode of education.

Froebel's own records of the birth of a baby provide him with the evidence that a child, only a few minutes old, is utterly helpless and that his only chance of survival is his self-activity. Froebel pays attention to the child's physical, emotional and intellectual development even at this early stage and observes that random gazing soon changed into purposeful action.[1] From the very beginning the child is involved in bringing order into the world into which he has been born.

At the beginning, the child feels himself undifferentiated and not separated from the world around him, thus his first endeavour is an attempt through the use of his limbs and senses to separate himself from and to order, this dark and chaotic world around him.[2]

The emphasis is again on the child's own action. The conclusions Froebel draws from these observations of the very young child are supported by philosophical arguments. Froebel reasons that every creature carries the characteristics of its creator. Man was created in the likeness of God. God, however, is life and this is expressed in creativity. Man's existence too is expressed during his life through his activity. The drive for activity is the first expression of the human being. 'The child, as a likeness of his creator, is a being who through his activity and then observation is led to full consciousness.'[3]

The order in which activity, observation and consciousness are mentioned is important (*Durch Schaffen zum Schauen, zum Bewusstsein*). We notice that it is the child's activity which provides him with the point of focus which in turn leads to knowledge. Froebel continues by saying that the processes of externalisation (activity) and internalisation (observation, reflection) are the same at any stage of development and therefore allows even the very young child to live a complete and purposeful life, preparing him for the realization of unity with his creator in later life.[4]

Like Piaget, Froebel found in the earliest sensory-motor activities of infants typical analogues of adult thought and behaviour. Froebel's notion that activity leads to observation and reflection and then to understanding is vitally different from Pestalozzi's notion of *Anschauung* (observation and reflection) leading to knowledge - a difference which has only been fully accepted since Piaget's work of the 1930s, where his observations of the origin of intelligence and reality constructions in his own three children focused on the child's actions in the course of encounters with objects, people and events.

Pestalozzi believed that sense-impressions were the foundation of all knowledge and that human powers developed by themselves, provided these sense-impressions were presented to children in an easy and definite sequence. At the same time he realized that sense data were experienced only in a confused way and to enable the mind to control its experiences, it was essential to give children instruction in language, form and number. These categories would enable the child to move from *Anschauung* (looking and observing) to *Begriff* (concept).

To Froebel perceptual knowledge was in itself insufficient not only because it was frequently misleading (e.g. size-weight relationship), but also because perceptual data was not productive of any educational value unless the mind had been prepared to receive the new perception. Only 'self-activity' could bring new knowledge into relationship with the old and verify any differences. Discrepancies between what was known and what was new would prompt the learner to ask the appropriate question. Adults were essential to this process, providing objects and material, guiding the activity and posing problems. But unless the child himself was aware that there was a problem, no learning could take place.

Piaget too arrived at the conclusion that actions are the basis for abstract thought. He says that unlike adults, who reason either deductively from the general to the particular or from the particular to the general, the child at the pre-operational stage reasons transductively from the particular to the particular. Though this may lead to valid conclusions, it frequently does not. Piaget reasons that further actions by the child will establish the truth or falsehood of his conclusions, establish equilibrium or disequilibrium between the processes of assimilation and accommodation, between the new and the old. It is the process between assimilation and accommodation which to Piaget explains the functioning of reversible operations which in turn lead to independent thought, and, he points out, these 'operations originate from actions'.[5]

Froebel's idea that the baby needs 'to separate himself from the environment' is again taken up when he talks about the three months old child who is now concentrating on separating self and object. It is a process which is painful to the child, for it involves 'having and not having', 'unity and separation'. Objects are not yet permanent and the only way we as adults can help the child to establish this most important concept, is by changing these situations frequently so that what is apparently lost, is also quickly found. We play with the child and play becomes pleasurable.

Froebel's notion that the origin of play is to be found in the adult's deliberate attempt to make the child's learning more acceptable seems to suggest that play is not something which is readily available to the child. It suggests that play has to be learned.

The child who is repeatedly presented with an object which then again is withdrawn and hidden from him, is involved in the discovery of wonder. So is the child who repeatedly bangs a tin lid on a saucepan, a wonder which indicates that we can be the source of effects which are seemingly beyond our power. Once the child realizes that the sound made on the saucepan is predictable and depends on the actions carried out, once he realizes that an object hidden will always be in its hiding-place, the characteristics of wonder and with it the incentive for play has gone. New play possibilities will have to be discovered. Learning to play, like any other learning, takes place in developmental stages and discovery is an important part of it. Froebel maintained that even the play of older children presupposed a certain stage of development, a certain ability.

> ... if there is enough space and children have sufficiently developed towards a quiet, sensible and continuous self-activity, the Gifts can be used for individual play where

every child does and plays as he wishes; but this presupposes . . . a certain stage of development.[6]

Though man's love of frequently repeating what he knows may be 'natural', the content of play has to be learned from those who know. Playing chess or bridge or indeed playing 'mothers and fathers', 'trains' or 'traffic policeman', demanded observation, reflection and restructuring which is akin to any other learning usually considered work, even if this kind of play is classified as 'imitation'. How clearly Froebel understood the value of 'imitative play', and how closely he linked it with the child's learning has been illustrated in detail. But even apparently simple exercises like throwing a ball for height and for distance were practised separately and 'then combined to a whole'.[7]

Because, to Froebel, the continuation of play depended on a low-level tension 'between the familiar and the new' and because children had to learn how to play, Froebel maintained that only an active and purposeful life in and out of school could produce rich play. Froebel had frequently observed that what children had learned in school they would later use in their play outside the classroom. It was therefore inevitable, in Froebel's thinking, that 'free play' had to lead to 'structured play' where the element of freedom and the element of structure, law and order provided the tension so essential for the continuation of that activity.

While working in Switzerland, Froebel was asked to produce a blue-print of a school for the education of the poor. He answered by stating in the first paragraph that the aim of any education, whether for the poor or the rich, must be the concern for a person as an active, feeling and thinking human being, an education that proceeds in unity and harmony with God, nature, mankind and self. But because Froebel's education was to a large extent based on self-activity, it was of the utmost importance that man was brought to the realization himself that there was unity in all diversity and that hidden laws existed even in apparently arbitrary phenomena. This was also Froebel's objective for play. It was the adult's task to lead children in their play in such a way that later they could discover these laws in their own play and subsequently in the reality of their own lives. Keeping this long-term goal well in mind, Froebel then concentrated on certain short-term goals which he considered essential, or at least helpful, in achieving his final goal. Such short-term goals might be concerned with 'the establishment of interest', 'the development of language', 'the experience of freedom and order in play', 'the development of concepts' etc. Here are some of Froebel's short-term goals as found in the description and explanation of the Gifts, Occupations and Mother Songs.

'I always start with the child' is a well-known dictum of Froebel's. It referred to the child's ability as well as to his interests. The story told by Middendorff and where Froebel joined the little girl's play with the Gifts, is an example of how much Froebel valued a child's interests as a means for learning.

Froebel's observation of children had established that children are continually looking for the 'new', for the unfamiliar, for 'change'. This was not necessarily something completely new, but the 'new in the old', the 'unfamiliar in the familiar', as for example in the different usage of the same object or the same activity with a different object. It followed that Froebel's Gifts, as well as the exercises to be carried out with the Gifts, had to be constructed in a way which incorporate the unfamiliar in the familiar. The soft ball of the first Gift was changed for the hard ball in the second Gift. To the wooden ball of the second Gift was added the wooden cube, because it was structurally the opposite of the sphere. Froebel believed that the teaching which used the 'unexpected' would not only create the element of surprise and maintain interest, but would also force the learner to pay attention to differences and that by careful comparison he would learn and understand.

But 'teaching by opposites' was not only based on psychological reasons. Froebel argued that life itself demonstrated the 'law of opposites' in every sphere and at every level. Mankind only existed because there were male and female; nature survived because icy winter was followed by the warm spring sun. When man had worked hard intellectually, his body demanded physical exercises; and man's 'inner life' demanded 'outward expression', just as external experiences demanded internalisation.

The child's activities too demand a constant change, but a change which was 'lawful'[8] and not arbitrary. Using the right hand when playing with the ball was followed by the use of the left hand and then both hands, just as order and a certain logic demanded that in the Movement Games the Visiting Games were followed by 'The Brook', 'The Mill' and finally 'The Wheel'. By using 'lawful changes', Froebel tried to avoid getting into conflict with the 'predictable learning situation', which he also considered essential for successful learning, for even surprise demanded recognition and therefore the element of predictability. Charlesworth in his paper 'The Role of Surprise in Cognitive Development' says that surprise implies an external stimulus which bears a particular relationship to the subject's cognitive structures which are

> . . . responsible for the production of expectancies that both aid the individual in responding to the stimulus . . . and determine the total physiological changes and overt responses that occur when the expected outcome of the stimulus circumstances is discordant with the stimulus circumstances themselves.[9]

Expectancy is essential for surprise to take place. Piaget's equilibration model of cognitive growth postulates the same condition.

The teaching of opposites, however, demanded a mediator. The notion of the mediator plays a considerable part in Froebel's writings and is based on the principle of 'dialectical synthesis' as found in the philosophy of romanticism. The unification of two apparently irreconcilable opposites can only be brought about by finding an entity (an object, an idea) which would bridge the differences. The ball, for example, is the mediator between the child and the outside world, for with it he can express what he knows, and learn what is still new to him. The Gifts mediate between children and parents, and the Kindergarten between children and society. The second Gift, which at first consisted of the wooden ball and wooden cube, was eventually extended to include the mediator, a cylinder. Froebel's basic educational aim, that of 'life-unity', can ultimately only come about by self-knowledge. Self-knowledge however is only made possible by standing outside oneself and comparing the self as it is, with the self as it ought to be. The self as it is, can only be judged by the actions which that self has performed so far. One's actions were therefore the mediator between one's true self and the self one aspired to be. Action, language, mathematics all were mediators and purposefully combined in their most elementary form in a child's play. For

> Play is a mediator between "want and ought". Genuine play is harmonious permeation in the child of what the child's drives want with what the (educational) laws demand.[10]

It is this alternating aspect in play which keeps the child on constant alert and made play, in Froebel's view, such an ideal medium for learning.

One of the most important skills a child had to learn was that of communication. Because few activities provided richer opportunities for the acquisition of language, Froebel insisted, that any play activity be accompanied by the 'explanatory word'. The verses which Froebel produced in conjunction with the Mother Songs and the Gifts could be learned off by heart, provided this did not create an obstacle to the main task which was the understanding of 'inner meaning and connections'. Froebel emphasised that the growth of language was not dependent on the learning of verses, but on intensive play with the Gifts or any other material to be found in the environment. The more objects a child created with his material, the greater the number of connections he would have to make, which in turn would lead to more complex ideas and therefore to the search for new words.

This idea was made even more explicit when Froebel said that talking to children was not primarily a matter of extending their vocabulary, but of helping them to focus on the important aspects of their environment. It was a tool to help children to perceive objects, their parts and their characteristics. The rich treasure of such experiences was the vehicle for the growth of language, just as a full and purposeful life was the basis for nourishing play.

Froebel believed that the accurate use of language assists memory,[11] is an essential medium for ascertaining the inner world of objects and then representing them,[12] leads to comparative thinking,[13] and demands judicious consideration and thoughtful representation.[14] Froebel, like Piaget, considered language as part of the symbolic function within the cognitive development of the child rather than as an independent 'object of knowing', and like Chomsky he puts the emphasis on the creative aspect of language.

Just as purposeful play encourages the development of language because the child is looking for the right word to supply meaning and establish inner connections in his play, so it is also true that meaningful language encourages play, especially if that language is a shared activity between peers. There are many references in Froebel's writings to the importance of social play. In a letter dated 10 July 1839, Froebel describes the functioning of his first Kindergarten. There were forty children aged one to six, but there were also some older children 'who were guides and real play-companions to their younger siblings'. G. Wells from Bristol University, who has carried out extensive research into children's language development, maintains that learning language and learning through language are co-extensive and that:

> some of the richest opportunities for talking and learning occur when child and adult are engaged in collaborative activity, such as carrying out household tasks, like cooking or cleaning.[15]

And Froebel certainly would have added 'play'.

This kind of 'teaching', whether of language or any other area of knowledge, was no longer a matter of transmitting sets of facts, but a matter of sharing experiences and exploring their meanings together. Therefore, the role of the teacher had to be redefined.

As the processes of education begin as soon as the child is born, and as the only teacher is available to a child of this age is its parents, parents, and especially mothers, had to take on the task of education in the first instance. When Froebel talks about the teacher, he includes any adult who is concerned with the upbringing and care of children, especially mothers. Equally, when he directs his explanations of the Gifts 'to mothers', he makes it explicit that this also includes teachers. The education of children had to go hand in hand with the education of parents. The Kindergarten had to be located in the centre of the village or town so that parents, especially mothers, had easy access to it to observe teachers working with the children. Parents would then be able to carry on the good work at home. They were encouraged to visit the Kindergarten at any time of the day and to take part in the games and exercises. They had to be taken into the teacher's confidence, just as parents had to trust the teachers, for the good of the child.

Not until now has there been scientific evidence that such co-operation between teachers and parents can influence a child's intellectual development enormously. The research done at the Froebel Institute in London shows how a two-year programme of rich educational provision for pre-school-age children, together with the close co-operation of their parents, increased the children's intelligence quota by an average of twenty per cent. Chris Athey's book *Extending Thought in Young Children* provides convincing evidence of the justification of Froebel's belief that a trusting, working relationship between parents and teachers is essential for the successful education of children.

Froebel's frequent references to non-interference with a child's activity, as for example in his insistence that each teacher must have his own set of Gifts, so as not to interrupt what a child is doing at a particular moment, have led to the belief that the teacher's task consists of preparing the ground, setting the scene and then retiring to the periphery so as not to intervene in the learning process. It is important to notice, that the reasons given for the non-interference are based on educational principles. Froebel argues that it will prevent interruption of a child's concentration and allow a child to persevere till the task has been completed. It is a *positive* action on the part of the teacher to encourage and foster the powers of concentration as well as the pursuit of a goal to its completion. But, and this is equally important, having observed the child's actions and endeavours, the teacher is now ready with his own set of Gifts to suggest to the child further possibilities.

To be able to indicate the possible next move, teachers need to have a complete overview of the material to be taught and have to be masters of their subjects, knowing more than the children at this stage could possibly need. Only teachers who understood Froebel's philosophy underlying the use of the Gifts could be aware of their educational possibilities, their structures and boundaries. Children had to investigate and comprehend the possibilities and limitations of the Gifts and this needed the knowledge and guidance of the teacher. At the same time teachers had to be well versed in the stages of development of children as well as with the total educational process. To know something about the children one taught without knowledge of what went before and what followed was not sufficient. Only when these three conditions: knowledge of the subject, knowledge of children's stages of development and knowledge of educational processes were satisfied, could a teacher decide with some confidence 'how', rather than 'when' to introduce new knowledge.

Equally important to Froebel were the means by which the material was to be imparted. Teachers should pay attention to the 'how' as well as to the 'what'. It had to be done in an orderly way where events were predictable and where the children's expectations could be utilised for learning. A child who knew what was going to happen the next day and the day after was mentally prepared to pay attention to the new material presented in a way which the unprepared mind could not do.

Froebel also emphasised that teachers had to work and play with the children because it created a genuine bond between teacher and taught, a bond which would promote respect for each other. A teacher (adult, parent) who participated in children's activities, talked to them and with them and who cared for their inner (mental, spiritual, emotional) life, would soon be recognised by the child as a person to be trusted. Froebel also believed that by working with children, teachers are all the time open to further learning from children, indicating to them how they should teach. This concept of 'learning through children' has sometimes been taken to mean 'learning with children', conveying the idea that a teacher is free to learn about the material to be presented to the children at their level and at the same time as the children. That this is a most serious misunderstanding is clear from what Froebel has said about the mastery of the subject to be taught. The idea of 'learning through children' however contains the notion that the teacher imparts attitudes about learning during the educational process, emphasising that education is an ongoing process rather than a state to be achieved.

To Froebel, then, a teacher was a person who was master of his subject, knowledgeable about children's stages of development and knowledgeable in the psychology of learning which made him competent in communicating his subject. He was also a person who had positive attitudes about teaching and learning and imparted these values during the educational process by the way he taught. Such teaching also demonstrated his attitude towards the notion of freedom in education. This was not merely a matter of taking note of the signs of the time, but of relating it to the learning processes in general.

When Froebel, by advocating the training of women teachers, drew upon himself the ridicule and anger of the profession, he was not concerned with supporting the women's movement, of which he was later accused, but with the one-sidedness of the upbringing of children. The educational process could not possibly be complete when 'the other half of humanity', as he called it, was conspicuous for its absence from the task of educating children.

Similarly, when Froebel advocated less interference with children's living and learning, he did not base his argument on the notion of *liberté* for its own sake, but on the experience that people, and that included children, are more receptive if they are co-operating by choice rather than participating through coercion. Froebel's account of the Folk and Youth Festival in Altenstein (1850) makes the point that only those who took part of their own free-will, will have been in the right frame of mind to grasp the meaning of the festival they were celebrating.

Of course, there were several other reasons why children should be allowed more freedom, but most important from the educator's point of view was the fact that life itself was an experience in the alternating actions of freedom and necessity and children had to be introduced to such important concepts, at an early age. No medium was better suited to the introduction of 'law and freedom' to young children than play, for play offered 'freedom within certain laws'. Thus, Froebel argued, play leads to self-discipline and to respect for order and authority. In play a child becomes aware of himself as an individual by virtue of the experience of freedom and choice, and becomes aware of the need for authority and order by virtue of his dependence on others and the limiting factors of the material he uses.

Freedom could never be bestowed upon people, including children, but had to be worked for, thought about, defined, sensed, discovered and appreciated. Freedom presupposed law and order in which it could operate, just as authority and the laws of necessity only became meaningful against the background and the alternative choice of freedom. Froebel demonstrated with the third Gift that this alternating pattern between freedom and the laws of necessity, observable in real life as well as in play, are also the basis for the creation of beauty.

Such freedom was especially essential, for teachers and children alike, when encouraging the creative aspects in a child's development. After all, man's progress depended on his venture into the unknown, his hunches and imagination and the use of the symbol and the surmise were essential tools in that process. The support and encouragement of the symbolic and the surmise, therefore, became one of Froebel's great educational aims.

'Play is a mirror of life', says the final edition of the explanations to the first Gift (1838); a mirror which reflected the players own life as well as life in general. When Froebel talks about the symbolic in play, we notice that he presented the symbolic meaning of play at two levels: the anthropological and the psychological. His references to the deeper meaning of life as found in play and as outlined in the essays on ice-skating and sledging give a clear indication that Froebel, like Huizinga and Schiller, saw in play something essentially belonging to man.

> Play . . . is not just a matter relating to physical and mental development, nor . . . merely a matter of satisfying the self-activity drive, but it originates from the direct demands of the humaneness of man and is directly related to it.[16]

Play at this level was essentially part of the characteristics of man. The child on the sledge who speeds towards the bottom of the hill without fear and without hesitation, is symbolically like the spirit of man moving towards his established goal. A person who recognised his goal, kept it in his mind and persevered until the goal was obtained exhibited self-reliance, independence and reflective thinking. Goal-orientated behaviour thus viewed was truly human in character and though not always available in real life, was certainly available in play. Play at this level of interpretation was anthropological, belonging to man as it could never belong to the activities of animals.

At the psychological level Froebel listed 'symbolic play' as the kind of activity where children re-created experiences from their own lives, so that the 'inner' life had to be represented by 'outer' actions. Froebel linked this representation of the child's inner life in play with the child's observation and internalisation of the outer world and the thoughtful comparison of them both. Play therefore is really a constant interaction between the inner and outer life of the child, just as work is a constant interaction between the inner and outer life of the adult, though we have to remember, of course, that the adult's work in Froebel's ideal world was an activity chosen by the adult as a means for expressing his talents rather than a job for earning money. This enabled Froebel to say that a child's play was his work, for the interaction which took place between the inner and the outer, whether at the level of the adult or the level of the child, were in both cases symbolic representations of the search for unity. Learning could take place when the child, or the adult, reflected on the differences between the inner and the outer. God, life, nature, work, all had these basic characteristics of the inner and the outer with the mediating agent between the two - and so did play.

Children, especially very young children, were not consciously aware of the symbolic in play, yet there was never any doubt in Froebel's mind that at least the presentiment for it must exist. Froebel argued that whatever man is eventually capable of doing, or thinking, must at least be present as a 'surmise' when he is a child. He pointed out that adults too must work at the level of the surmise when interpreting the symbolic before it can be fully grasped intellectually. Equally it is in the surmise that we can get some idea of the notion of constructing the whole from its parts. To observe without reflection was 'empty observation' and could never lead to real understanding. Previous knowledge will of course help to direct our thinking, but unless we make use of our ability to probe into the dark, unless we foster the hunch and pay attention to presentiments, human progress would soon be stunted.

Einstein too placed the driving force of the sciences into the realm of the surmise, when he said:

> The most beautiful and the most profound emotion is the sensation of the mystical: it is the power of all true science. To know that what is impenetrable really exists is at the centre of true religiousness.[17]

Froebel, like most of the Romantics, perceived God in the action of man, in life and in nature, all of which therefore achieved symbolic meaning. And because to him 'education' was the highest form of human activity and children's existence in the strange world of adults could not possibly be made intelligible by rational argument, it became quite clear that the symbol had to be used as an educational aid.

Froebel used the words *Sinnbild* and *Gegenbild* more often than the word 'symbol'. A *Sinnbild* is like an emblem and the *Gegenbild* like a mirror-image. The emblem emphasises the pictorial expression of the mind, the movement from the 'inner to the outer', while the mirror-image is a more 'natural symbol', a symbol which exists but needs recognition, it is a movement from the 'outer to the inner'. Froebel further differentiated between 'example', 'copy', 'original' or archetype, and 'sign',[18] illustrating that Froebel's many references to the symbolic as a means for learning was based on the prolonged and deep study of the problem.

The symbol and the surmise fulfil in the final analysis the same function. They are both tools which above all are to be used to discover ourselves and therefore ultimately the meaning of life. Everything else which children learn in their play - language, knowledge about people and objects, co-operation etc. - are all subordinated to these greater aims.

Just as every single experience of a presentiment, a surmise, must eventually converge towards the surmise of the total image of this world, so it is the religious presentiment, above all others, which will lead man to the 'Experience of the Unity with his Creator'. The fostering of the surmise in young children started with the baby in arms and enabled Froebel to introduce abstract notions like freedom, respect for others, honesty, etc. at a concrete level starting with finger-games and nursery rhymes. It is in the area of 'the symbol and the surmise' that Froebel has attracted his major critics and where he is least understood. It is also this area which has not yet been brought to the attention of educational research today.

1. Froebel, 1838, MS 18/4/8.
2. ibid, 1845, MS 19/8/122-127, p.9.
3. ibid, 1842, MS 8/47/29-94, p.43.
4. Froebel, 1842, MS 8/47/29-94, p.44.
5. Piaget *in* De Cecco, 1969, p.273.
6. Froebel, 1841, MS 1/7/24-53.
7. ibid, 1840, MS 18/5/1/1-57, p.47.
8. ibid, 1842, MS 8/47/29-94.
9. Elkind & Flavell, 1970, p.278.
10. Froebel, 1845, MS 19/8/5/122-127.
11. Froebel, 1844, MS 19/8/2/9.
12. ibid, 1845, MS 19/8/122-127, p.12.

13. ibid, 1850, MS 19/9/2/107-121, p.6.
14. ibid, 1851, MS 19/9/88, p.4.
15. G. Wells *in* Cohen & Cohen, 1988, p.121.
16. Froebel *in* Lange, 1863, p.380.
17. Einstein *in* Cluny, 1963, p.156.
18. Heiland, 1967, p.12.

# Bibliography

Manuscripts are listed first. The numerals are taken from the MS as found in the archives of the Deutsche Akademie der Wissenschaften in East Berlin.

A Kindergarten teacher, 1847, MS 21/20/0
A Kindergarten teacher, 1850, MS 21/23/103
Erdmann, C. & Michaelis M., 1839, MS 21/20 Letztes Stueck
Foelsing, J., 1848, MS 7/42/25-29
Froebel, F., nd, MS 1/1/12
    1841, MS 1/7/24-53
    1831, MS 5/29/13-14
    nd, MS 5/29/79
    nd, MS 6/33
    nd, MS 7/40/20-21
    nd, MS 7/41/194-195
    1842, MS 8.47.29-94
    1842, MS 12/1/8
    1812, MS 15/5/5/1/11
    1821, MS 17/-
    1838, MS 18/4/5
    1838, MS 18/4/8
    1838, MS 18/ab.4/F.5,
    1837, MS 18/4/17
    1840, MS 18/5/1/1-57
    nd, MS 18/7/5/155-156
    nd, MS 18/7/5/168-174
    1839, MS 18/8/8a
    1844, MS 19/8/2
    1844, MS 19/8/2/9
    nd, MS 19/8/4

1845, MS 19/8/4/136-137f
1845, MS 19/8/5/122-127
1845, MS 19/8/6/175i-175p
1839, MS 19/8/8a (Blatt 102, 103)
1849, MS 19/8/8c/143-151
1851, MS 19/8/8f
1850, MS 19/9/2/107-121
1830, MS 19/9/5/159-160
1851, MS 19/12/1
nd, MS 19/12/2/21-26
Froebel, L., nd, MS 3/15b/274
Home and Colonial, nd, MS 8/46/19-20
Infant School Society, nd, MS 8/46/19-20
A short account of the Institution for Infant School Teachers and the Model Infant
    School, Gray's Inn Road. No Date, probably 1843
Levin, L., nd, MS 3/15/374
Seele I., nd, MS 33/142-178
Reports: 1839, MS 21/20/0 Opening of a Kindergarten
    1848, MS 7/43/76-97 Teachers Conference, Rudolstadt
    1851, MS 21/22/1 Teachers Conference, Liebenstein


Annis, P.N., 'A Study of the Participation, Imitative Behaviour and Play of Three
    to Seven Year old Children during and after Exposure to selected TV Pro-
    grammes.' M.Ed. Thesis, University of Leicester, 1971.
Athey, C., *Extending Thought in Young Children*, London, (Paul Chapman, 1990).
Bantock, G.H., *Freedom and Authority in Education,* London, (Faber & Faber,
    1952).
Bantock, G.H., *Education, Culture and the Emotions,* London, (Faber & Faber,
    1967).
Bantock, G.H., *Culture, Industrialisation and Education*, London, (Routledge &
    Kegan Paul, 1968).
Bantock, G.H., *Dilemmas of the Curriculum*, Oxford, (Martin Robertson, 1980).
Barbizet, J., *Human Memory and its Pathology*, San Francisco, (Freeman & Co,
    1970).
Barnard, H. (Ed.), 'Papers on Froebel's Kindergarten', *American Journal of
    Education*, Hartford, 1881.
Bennett, J.G., *The Dramatic Universe*, London, (Hodder & Stoughton, 1966).
Blochmann, E., *Froebel's theorie des Spieles*, Weinheim, I. (Beltz, 1965).
Bode, M., 'Friedrich Froebel's Erziehungsidee und ihre Grundlage' *Zeitschrift für
    Geschichte der Erziehung und des Unterrichtes*, Berlin, 1925, Vol. 15, p. 118-
    182.
Bollnow, O.F., *Die Paedagogik der deutschen Romantik*, 2nd ed., Stuttgart,
    (Kohlhammer, 1967).

Bowen, H.C., *Froebel and Education by Self-Activity,* London, (Heinemann, 1893).

Boyd, W., *Emile for Today,* 2nd ed., London, (Heinemann, 1964).

Brearley, M. & Hitchfield, E., *A Teacher's Guide to Reading Piaget,* London, (Routledge & Kegan Paul, 1966).

Brubacher, J.S., *Modern Philosophies of Education,* 2nd ed., London, (McGraw Hill, 1969).

Bruner, J.S., *Towards a Theory of Instruction,* Cambridge, Mass, (Harvard University Press, 1966).

Buytendijk, F.J.J., *Wesen und Seins des Spieles,* Berlin, (Karl Wolf Verlag, 1933).

Castle, E.B., *The Teacher,* London, (Oxford University Press, 1970).

Caxton, P.P., *Sketches of Froebel's Life & Time,* Springfield, Mass, (Milton Bradley, 1914).

Chalke, R.D., *A Synthesis of Froebel and Herbart,* London, (University Tutorial Press, 1912).

Clarke, C.P.S., *A Short History of the Christian Church,* 2nd ed., London, (Longman, 1950).

Cohen, A & Cohen L. (Eds), *Early Education: The Pre-School Years,* London, (Chapman, 1988).

Comenius, J.A., *Selections,* Introd. by J. Piaget, Paris, (Unesco, 1957).

Cox, C.B. & Boyson, R. (Eds), *Black Paper 1975,* London, (Dent & Sons, 1975).

Copleston, F., *A History of Philosophy,* Vol. VII, London, (Burns & Oates, 1963).

Cranston, M., *Freedom. A New Analysis,* London, (Longman, Green & Co., 1953).

Cuny, H., *Albert Einstein the Man,* London, (Souvenir Press, 1963).

Curtis, A.M., *A Curriculum for the Pre-School Child,* Windsor, (NFER-Nelson, 1986).

Dearden, R.F., *The Philosophy of Primary Education,* London, (Routledge & Kegan Paul, 1968).

Dearden, R.F., Hirst, P.H. & Peters, R.S., *Education and the Development of Reason,* London, (Routledge and Kegan Paul, 1972).

De Cecco, J.P., *The Psychology of Language, Thought and Instruction,* London, (Holt, Rinehardt & Winston, 1969).

Desforges, C.W. (Ed.), *Early Childhood Education,* Edinburgh, (Scottish Academic Press, 1989).

Elkind, D. & Flavell, J.H., *Studies in Cognitive Development,* 2nd ed., New York, (Oxford University Press, 1970).

Erikson, E.H., *Childhood and Society,* New York, (Norton, 1950).

Flavell, J.H., *The Development Psychology of Jean Piaget,* New York, (Van Nostrand Co., 1963).

Freire, P., *Cultural Action for Freedom,* Harmondsworth, (Penguin, 1972).

Friedmann, M. (Ed.), *The Knowledge of Man,* London, (Allen & Unwin, 1965).

Froebel, F., *Kommt lasst uns unseren Kindern Leben Anleitung zum Gebrauch . . . der ausgefuehrten dritten Gabe . . . .,* Blankenburg, (Anstalt zur Pflege des Beschaeftigungs triebes der Kindheit & Jugend, 1844).

Gahagen, D.M. & G.H., *Talk Reform*, London, (Routledge & Kegan Paul, 1970).

Giel, K., *Fichte und Froebel*, Heidelberg, (Quelle & Meyer, 1959).

Goldman, R., *Readiness for Religion*, London, (Routledge & Kegan Paul, 1965).

Green, F.C., *Jean-Jacques Rousseau: a study of his life and writings*, Cambridge, (Cambridge University Press, 1955).

Halfter, F., *Friedrich Froebel. Der Werdegang eines Menschenerziehers*, Halle, (1931).

Hanschmann, A.B., *Friedrich Froebel. Die Entwicklung seiner Erziehungsidee in seinen Leben*, Eisenach, (Bacmeister Verlag, 1875).

Hayward, F.H., *The Educational Ideas of Pestalozzi and Froebel*, London, (Ralph, Holland & Co., 1905).

Heafford, M.R., *Pestalozzi*, London, (Methuen & Co., 1967).

Heiland, H., *Die Symbolwelt Friedrich Froebel's*, Heidelberg, (Quelle & Meyer, 1967).

Heiland, H., *Literatur und Trends in der Froebelforschung*, Weinheim, (Beltz Verlag, 1972).

Heiland, H. (Ed.), *Friedrich Froebel. Ausgewaehlte Schriften*, Dusseldorf, (Knepper, 1974).

Herron, R.E. & Sutton-Smith, B., *Child's Play*, New York, (John Wiley & Sons, 1971).

Hirst, P.H. & Peters, R.S., *The Logic of Education*, London, (Routledge & Kegan Paul, 1970).

Hoffmann, E. (Ed.), *Friedrich Froebel und Karl Hagen*, Weimar, (Werden & Wirken, 1948).

Hoffmann, E. (Ed.), *Froebel's Theorie des Spieles, III*, Weinheim, (Beltz, 1967).

Hoffmann, E. (ed.), *Friedrich Froebel Ausgewaehlte Schriften*, Düsseldorf, (Verlag Helmut Küpper, 1964).

Huizinga, J., *Homo Ludens*, 3. Auflage, Basel, Brussels, Köln, Wien, (Akademische Verlagsanstalt Pantheon Verlag für Geschichte und Politik, 1951).

Huizinga, J., *Homo Ludens*, London, (Routledge & Kegan Paul, 1944).

Hyde, D.M.G., *Piaget and Concept Development*, London, (Holt, Rinehart & Winston, 1970).

Inhelder, B. & Piaget, J., *The Early Growth of Logic in the Child*, London, (Routledge & Kegan Paul, 1964).

Kant, J., *Über Paedagogik*, Berlin, Akademie Ausgabe, Band 9, 1923.

King, E.J., *The Education of Teachers*, London, (Holt, Rinehart & Winston, 1970).

Klafki, W., *Das Paedagogische Problem des Elementaren und die Theorie der kategorialen Bildung*, Weinheim, (Beltz, 1959).

Klostermann, H. (Ed.), *Froebel's Theorie des Spiels, II*, 2nd ed., Langensalza, (Beltz, 1966).

Koehler, W., *The Task of Gestalt Psychology*, Princeton, (Princeton University Press, 1972).

Koestler, A., *The Act of Creation*, London, (Hutchinson, 1964).

Elkind, D. & Flavell, J.H., *Studies in Cognitive Development*, 2nd ed., New York, (Oxford University Press, 1970).

Erikson, E.H., *Childhood and Society*, New York, (Norton, 1950).

Flavell, J.H., *The Development Psychology of Jean Piaget*, New York, (Van Nostrand Co., 1963).

Freire, P., *Cultural Action for Freedom*, Harmondsworth, (Penguin, 1972).

Friedmann, M. (Ed.), *The Knowledge of Man*, London, (Allen & Unwin, 1965).

Froebel, F., *Kommt lasst uns unseren Kindern Leben Anleitung zum Gebrauch . . . der ausgefuehrten dritten Gabe . . . .*, Blankenburg, (Anstalt zur Pflege des Beschaeftigungs triebes der Kindheit & Jugend, 1844).

Gahagen, D.M. & G.H., *Talk Reform*, London, (Routledge & Kegan Paul, 1970).

Giel, K., *Fichte und Froebel*, Heidelberg, (Quelle & Meyer, 1959).

Goldman, R., *Readiness for Religion*, London, (Routledge & Kegan Paul, 1965).

Green, F.C., *Jean-Jacques Rousseau: a study of his life and writings*, Cambridge, (Cambridge University Press, 1955).

Halfter, F., *Friedrich Froebel. Der Werdegang eines Menschenerziehers*, Halle, (1931).

Hanschmann, A.B., *Friedrich Froebel. Die Entwicklung seiner Erziehungsidee in seinen Leben*, Eisenach, (Bacmeister Verlag, 1875).

Hayward, F.H., *The Educational Ideas of Pestalozzi and Froebel*, London, (Ralph, Holland & Co., 1905).

Heafford, M.R., *Pestalozzi*, London, (Methuen & Co., 1967).

Heiland, H., *Die Symbolwelt Friedrich Froebel's*, Heidelberg, (Quelle & Meyer, 1967).

Heiland, H., *Literatur und Trends in der Froebelforschung*, Weinheim, (Beltz Verlag, 1972).

Heiland, H. (Ed.), *Friedrich Froebel. Ausgewaehlte Schriften*, Dusseldorf, (Knepper, 1974).

Herron, R.E. & Sutton-Smith, B., *Child's Play*, New York, (John Wiley & Sons, 1971).

Hirst, P.H. & Peters, R.S., *The Logic of Education*, London, (Routledge & Kegan Paul, 1970).

Hoffmann, E. (Ed.), *Friedrich Froebel und Karl Hagen*, Weimar, (Werden & Wirken, 1948).

Hoffmann, E. (Ed.), *Froebel's Theorie des Spieles, III*, Weinheim, (Beltz, 1967).

Hoffmann, E. (ed.), *Friedrich Froebel Ausgewaehlte Schriften*, Düsseldorf, (Verlag Helmut Küpper, 1964).

Huizinga, J., *Homo Ludens*, 3. Auflage, Basel, Brussels, Köln, Wien, (Akademische Verlagsanstalt Pantheon Verlag für Geschichte und Politik, 1951).

Huizinga, J., *Homo Ludens*, London, (Routledge & Kegan Paul, 1944).

Hyde, D.M.G., *Piaget and Concept Development*, London, (Holt, Rinehart & Winston, 1970).

Inhelder, B. & Piaget, J., *The Early Growth of Logic in the Child*, London, (Routledge & Kegan Paul, 1964).

Kant, J., *Über Paedagogik*, Berlin, Akademie Ausgabe, Band 9, 1923.

King, E.J., *The Education of Teachers*, London, (Holt, Rinehart & Winston, 1970).

Klafki, W., *Das Paedagogische Problem des Elementaren und die Theorie der kategorialen Bildung*, Weinheim, (Beltz, 1959).

Klostermann, H. (Ed.), *Froebel's Theorie des Spiels, II*, 2nd ed., Langensalza, (Beltz, 1966).

Koehler, W., *The Task of Gestalt Psychology*, Princeton, (Princeton University Press, 1972).

Koestler, A., *The Act of Creation*, London, (Hutchinson, 1964).

Kuntze, M.A., *Friedrich Froebel. Sein Leben und sein Werk*, Heidelberg, (Quelle & Meyer, 1952).

Lange, W., *Aus Froebel's Leben und erstem Streben*, Berlin, (Enslin, 1862).

Lange, W., *Ideen Friedrich Froebel's über die Menschenerziehung*, Berlin, (Enslin, 1863).

Lange, W., *Friedrich Froebel's Gesammelte Paedagogische Schriften. Die Paedagogik des Kindergartens*, Berlin, (Enslin, 1874).

Lawrence, E. (Ed.), *Friedrich Froebel and English Education*, 2nd ed., London, (Routledge & Kegan Paul, 1969).

Lilley, I.M., *Friedrich Froebel. A Selection of his Writings*, London, (Cambridge University Press, 1967).

Lodge, R., *The Great Thinkers*, London, (Routledge & Kegan Paul, 1949).

Lomas, P., *True and False Experience*, London, (Allen Lane, 1949).

MacCormac, R.C., *Environment and Planning*, London, (1974).

Marenholtz-Bülow, *Erinnerungen an Friedrich Froebel*, Wigand Kassel, (1876).

Marenholtz-Bülow, *Reminiscences of Friedrich Froebel*, Trans. by Mann, London, (Central School Depot, nd).

Meredith, J.C. (Ed.), *Emanuel Kant. The Critique of Judgement*, London, (Oxford University Press, 1952).

Michaelis, E. & Moore, H.K., *Autobiography of Friedrich Froebel*, 2nd ed, London, (Allen & Unwin, 1915).

Michaelis, E. & Moore, H.K., *Froebel's Letters on the Kindergarten*, London, (Swan Sonnenschein & Co., 1891).

Morrish, I., *Education Since 1800*, London, (Allen & Unwin, 1970).

Nash, P., Kazamias, A.M. & Perkinson, H.J., *The Educated Man*, New York, (Wiley & Sons, 1965).

Nixon, M., *Children's Classification Skills*, (Australian Council for Ed. Research, 1971).

O'Conner, D.J., *A Critical History of Western Philosophy*, London, (Free Press of Glencoe, Collier-MacMillan, 1964).

Opie, I. & P., *Children's Games in Street and Playground*, London, (Oxford University Press, 1969).

Peters, R.S., *The Concept of Education*, London, (Routledge & Kegan Paul, 1967).

Piaget, J., *Play, Dreams and Imitation in Childhood*, 2nd ed., London, (Routledge & Kegan Paul, 1962).

Piaget, J., *The Origin of Intelligence in the Child*, London, (Routledge & Kegan Paul, 1953).

Piaget, J., *Six Psychological Studies*, New York, (Random House, 1968).

Piaget, J., *Science of Education and the Psychology of the Child*, London, (Longman, 1970).

Piaget, J. & Inhelder, B., *The Child's Conception of Space*, London, (Routledge & Kegan Paul, 1953).

Piaget, J. & Inhelder, B, *The Psychology of the Child*, 2nd ed., London, (Routledge & Kegan Paul, 1971).

Polanyi, M., *Knowing and Being*, London, (Routledge & Kegan Paul, 1969).

Pruefer, J., *Vorlaeufer Froebel's*, Langensalza, (Beyer & Soehne, 1911).

Pruefer, J. (Ed.), *Friedrich Froebel*, Leipzig, (Mutter & Koselieder, 1927).

Rinke, A., 'Friedrich Froebel's Philosophische Entwicklung,' *in* Mann's *Paedagogische Magazin*, Langensalza, (Beyer & Soehne, 1935).

Robinson, W.P., *Language and Social Behaviour*, Harmondsworth, (Penguin, 1972).

Robottom, J., *A Social and Economic History of Industrial Britain*, London, (Longman, 1986).

Rowse, A.L., *The Elizabethan Renaissance*, London, (MacMillan, 1972).

Russel, B., *History of Western Philosophy*, 2nd ed., London, (Allen & Unwin, 1965).

Scheuerl, H., *Beitraege zur Theorie des Spiels*, 2nd ed., Weinheim, (Beltz, 1969).

Schools Council Working Paper 44, *Religious Education in Primary Schools*, London, (Evans/Methuen Educational, 1972).

Schuffenhauer, H., *Friedrich August Wilhelm Froebel*, Berlin, (Volk & Wissen, 1962).

Schumacher, E.F., 'The Roots of Violence' *New Era*, Vol. 54, No. 1. (Jan/Feb 1973).

Seidel, F. (Ed.), *Friedrich Froebel Paedagogische Schriften* (3 Vols) *I Die Menschenerziehung, II Das Kindergartenwesen, III Mutter und Koselieder*, Leipzig, Wien, (Pichler Witwe & Sohn, 1883).

Seidel, F., *Mutter und Koselieder*, Trans. F. & E. Ford, London, (1895).

Spranger, E., *Aus Friedrich Froebel's Gedankenwelt*, Heidelberg, (Quelle & Meyer, 1964).

Stead, W.T. (Ed.), *Songs and Games*, London, (Books for the Bairns Office, 1905).

Stewart, W.A.C., *Progressives and Radicals in English Education*, London, (MacMillan, 1972).

Thompson, K., *Education and Philosophy*, Oxford, (Blackwell, 1972).

Thorpe, W.H., *Learning and Instincts in Animals*, London, (Methuen, 1956).

Van der Eyken, W. (ed.), *Education, The Child and Society; a documentary history 1900-1973*, Harmondsworth, (Penguin, 1973).

Vygotsky, L.S., *Mind in Society*, Los Angeles, (University of California Press, 1978).

Whitbread, N., *The Evolution of the Nursery-Infant School*, London, (Routledge & Kegan Paul, 1972).

# INDEX

# FOUNDATIONS OF PROGRESSIVE EDUCATION
## The History of the National Froebel Society

### JOACHIM LIEBSCHNER

This is the inspiring story of how a handful of people radically changed British education. These people, mostly young women, were members of the National Froebel Society, which tried to put into practice the educational philosophy and principles of Friedrich Froebel.

Following his ideas, they believed in the importance of every child, of whatever ability, that a child's intellectual, spiritual and physical development came about through the child's own endeavours, and that play was an integral part of the learning process. The author describes how, with the founding of the Kindergarten Movement in Great Britain, children's lives were to be revolutionised, and he provides for the first time a coherent picture of the lasting influences of these gentle young teachers.

*B/w illustrations, 234 x 156mm, hardback*
*176 pages, £19.50 net*
*ISBN 0 7188 2835 6*
*Published December 1991*